150 Best Tiny Home Ideas

150 Best Tiny Home Ideas

Manel Gutiérrez Couto

HARPER
DESIGN
An Imprint of HarperCollins Publishers

150 BEST TINY HOME IDEAS
Copyright © 2016 by LOFT Publications

HarperCollins books may be purchased for educational, business, or sales promotional use.
For information, please write the Special Markets Department at SPsales@harpercollins.com.

First published in 2016 by:
Harper Design
An Imprint of HarperCollins*Publishers*
195 Broadway
New York, NY 10007
Tel.: (212) 207-7000
Fax: (855) 746-6023
harperdesign@harpercollins.com
www.hc.com

Distributed throughout the world by:
HarperCollins*Publishers*
195 Broadway
New York, NY 10007

Editorial coordinator: Claudia Martínez Alonso
Art director: Mireia Casanovas Soley
Editor and texts: Manel Gutiérrez Couto
Layout: Cristina Simó Perales

ISBN 978-0-06-244466-0

Library of Congress Control Number: 2015960140

Printed in China
First printing, 2016

CONTENTS

INTRODUCTION

Small-scale homes have long proven to be an attractive and practical design solution for natural spaces located on the periphery of the city. Small chalets have become hugely popular, largely thanks to two key principles: despite their small space they benefit from all the basic commodities of any home, and they provide ample opportunity for direct contact with nature. And all this comes hand in hand with a huge respect for their natural environment.

It was the very popularity of these properties that saw them breaking geographical boundaries and settling themselves in areas that were far from their natural environment. These days, the spatial limitations of these types of homes make them suitable for far more than one single location. The most up-to-date designs can be adapted to situations ranging from city to mountain and coast.

This book takes us on a journey through the most current and breathtaking compact homes in existence in the world today, designed by the most talented architects and designers.

Over the course of four chapters, you will discover everything: classic cottages that have been passed through the filter of modernity; the most original space-saving solutions for urban locations; coastal houses perched in the most privileged of positions; and the most original, yet ever more commonplace, prefabricated and modular housing solutions.

In demanding environments such as the countryside or mountains, small chalets or cottages remain an ideal choice. These days, progress and developments in techniques, materials, and finishes, together with continuous experimentation and design innovation, have resulted in solutions that are completely in tune with their environment while retaining their every comfort and refined aesthetic finish.

The added attraction of a house simply by dint of its proximity to water, whether it be a river, lake, or ocean setting, is undeniable. Houses located by the water certainly enjoy a privileged position and especially in built-up coastal zones, thanks to their smaller size, manage to stamp their footprint on land where there is little room for construction. Moreover, these homes also demonstrate innovative strategies to help them adapt to the environmental conditions of their natural surroundings, such as the coast.

In urban environments, embracing small-scale designs has been something of a necessity. The growing demands on increasingly urbanized and highly populated spaces have led to the emergence of more and more intelligent living solutions. Today the aim is to get the most out of the little space available, without affecting the house's overall comfort. Moreover, in the same way as rural homes, urban houses also need to demonstrate a strong relationship with their immediate surroundings.

This book has also set aside a special space in which to showcase modular and prefabricated homes. Among these you will find everything from individual tiny homes that are fully mobile and equipped with the basic essentials for everyday life, to modular homes that despite their simple configuration create fully fledged small-scale residences that can be combined with other modules to create large-scale homes with every creature comfort. This type of house does more than just play with size; it demonstrates certain characteristics that set it apart from the crowd: easy transportation, practical installation in just about any location, minimal environmental impact, and low costs and energy bills.

The wide range of examples of tiny houses that are showcased in this book demonstrates that this is more than a mere architectural trend, more than a simple fad, but rather a phenomenon that is becoming more and more common and is not consigned to a single geographical area. Tiny houses are accessible and are adaptable to any environment, no matter how small and how demanding it may be. Living in small space, whether it be in a compact or a modular home, is no longer a handicap, nor does it require us to give up any of the creature comforts we would expect from a home of a larger size.

Countryside

The design of this house, perched on a plot that was bought by the owners some forty years ago, was driven both by the small size of the land and the legal restrictions on building in the area. The first floor is about six feet above the ground and the maximum height is no greater than twenty-five feet.

This 600-square-foot property explores a geometric solution that brings luxury to a minimal space. Despite its limited size, the experience and functions of this house are similar to those of any of the larger neighboring houses.

Beach Hampton
600 sq ft

Bates Masi + Architects

Amagansett, New York,
United States

© Bates Masi + Architects

Upper level floor plan

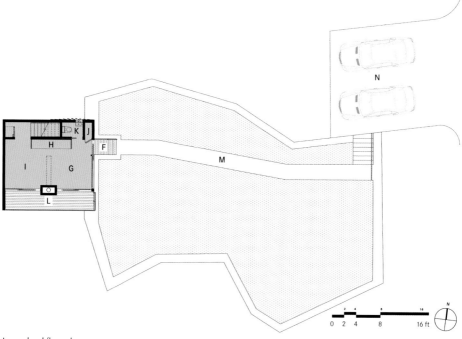

Lower level floor plan

N

0   2   4   8   16 ft

A. Laundry closet   H. Kitchen
B. Bathroom   I. Living room
C. Hall   J. Coat closet
D. Bedroom   K. Powder
E. Open to below   L. Deck
F. Entry   M. Entry walkway
G. Dining room   N. Parking

At the end of the access road through the native vegetation, this house is situated in the center of the landscape like an object mounted on a pedestal.

001

Open-plan spaces—those that incorporate different rooms within the same environment—tend to be a smart solution for use in compact homes.

Orientating the building correctly can eliminate the need for heating or air conditioning. In tiny houses, it can also ensure the interior is adequately lit.

Using large, transparent glass walls to separate certain spaces in place of walls creates the feeling of one continuous space.

This design is a response to the owner's wish to own a compact chalet that is easy to maintain and virtually indestructible; a place in which he and his wife can stay during his beloved fishing trips.

Supported by four steel columns, the chalet boasts a spectacular sliding gate that can be completely closed when the owner is away. The chalet's sturdy patina and raw materiality respond to the surrounding wilderness, while its verticality provides a safe haven from the occasional flooding of the nearby river.

Sol Duc Cabin
350 sq ft

Olson Kundig Architects

Olympic Peninsula, Washington, United States

© Benjamin Benschneider

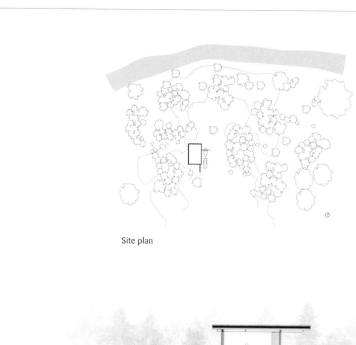

Site plan

West section

South section

Tiny houses are ideal for use in harsh natural environments. They can be easily raised on pillars to stand them away from the ground, and can have high ceilings attached to provide protection from the sun or storms.

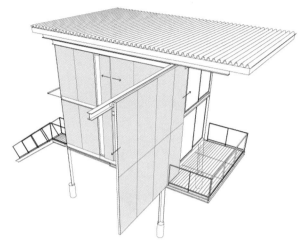

Axonometric view

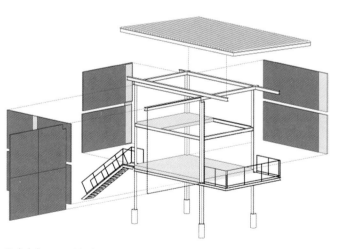

Exploded axonometric view

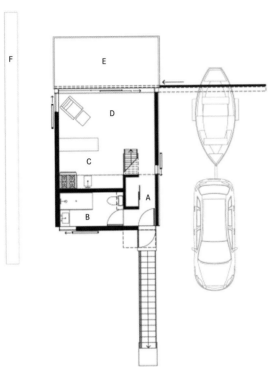

Main level plan

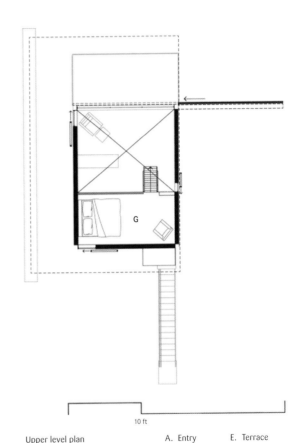

Upper level plan

|————————————⌐___⌐————————————|
10 ft

A. Entry   E. Terrace
B. Bathroom   F. Trench drain
C. Kitchen   G. Loft
D. Dining/
   Living room

In homes with high ceilings, installing a mezzanine not only makes the most of the height, it can also create little areas with much more privacy than the communal spaces.

This project is a prime example of the measures that are necessary for a house to coexist in total harmony with its surroundings. Through its structure and the materials used, it achieves a complete balance between the wishes of the clients, a small budget, and the role of the environment as an active agent in the final configuration of the project.

The result is a house that, by observing its landscape, maintains intact each and every tree that surrounds it (from roots to crown) without compromising the beautiful views that surround it as well.

Moose Road Residence
1,894 sq ft

Mork Ulnes Architects

Ukiah, California, United States

© Bruce Damonte

Made of raw, unfinished steel, the building's exterior cladding changes color and takes on a life of its own during the course of the day according to the movement of the sun.

006

Distributing a house into differently orientated axes enables it to be adapted to the peculiarities of the terrain and be divided into very distinct spaces.

007

High-intensity, white artificial lighting in the kitchen not only provides plenty of illumination under which to work, it also increases the feeling of space.

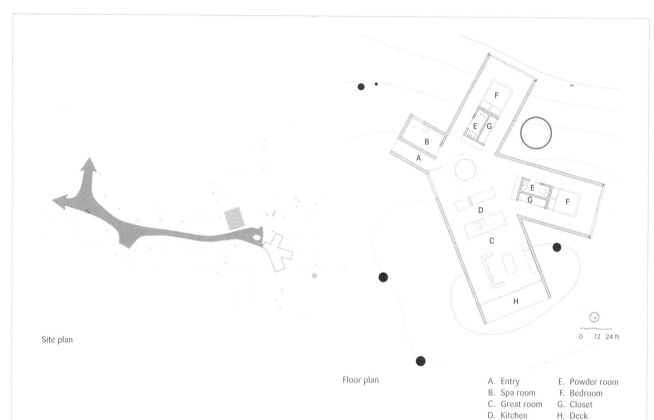

Site plan

Floor plan

A. Entry
B. Spa room
C. Great room
D. Kitchen

E. Powder room
F. Bedroom
G. Closet
H. Deck

0   12   24 ft

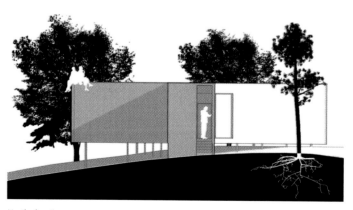

North elevation

Section

008

Brightly colored floors, especially those in the same color as the walls or one that is very similar, create continuity between surfaces, which immediately increases the feeling of space.

This project aimed to make the most of the reduced size of a home situated on a smaller than usual uncultivated plot. Thus, with just two full-height walls, the design creates an interior that is almost as big as the building's footprint. Furthermore, high ceilings and abundant natural light help to give the house a strong loft feel.

The end result is a reversal of expectations, in which the smallest house in fact contains the largest space: the square feet it lacks are made up for in volume.

BIG & small HOUSE
1,200 sq ft

**Simon Storey/
Anonymous Architects**

Los Angeles, California,
United States

© Steve King

009

When building on slopes and uneven terrain, constructing on piles helps to keep the plot intact and means that the entire space between the house and the ground beneath can be used.

Site plan

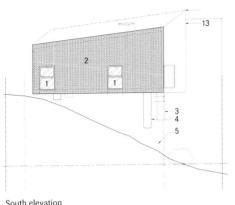

South elevation

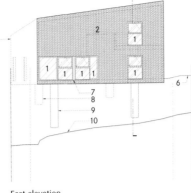

East elevation

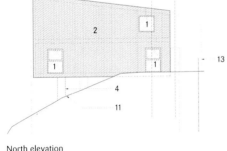

North elevation

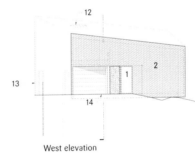

West elevation

1. Tempered glass, typical
2. Metal siding typical
3. Concrete pile beyond
4. Concrete pile, typical
5. Natural grade
6. Top of slope beyond
7. Structural post
8. Structural concrete pier beyond, typical
9. Structural concrete pier
10. Natural undisturbed finish grade
11. Natural finish grade
12. Skylight
13. Building beyond
14. Automatic sectional garage door

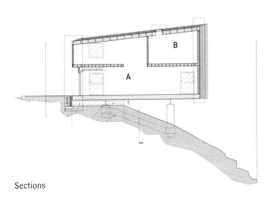

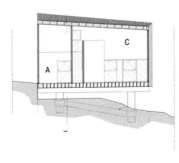

Sections

A. Garage
B. Mezzanine
C. Living room

Whether it be with natural or artificial light, effective lighting in passageways adds to the feeling of space and facilitates people's movement.

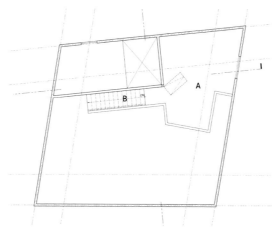

Loft plan

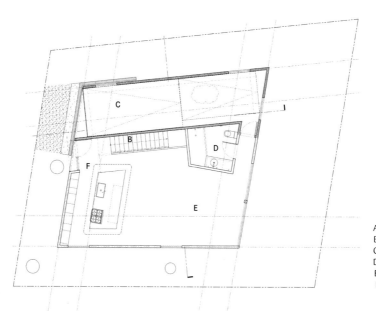

First floor plan

A. Bedroom
B. Stairs
C. Garage
D. Bathroom
E. Living/Dining room
F. Kitchen

011

Kitchen islands are a beautiful and practical way to provide continuity between the dining room and kitchen, as long as you have enough space to install them.

The house's asymmetric parallelogram footprint mimics the shape of the plot, and results in an unusual geometry inside and outside. The elevation of the house also reflects its shape.

012

It is difficult to get full use from corners. One way is to position the furniture so as to create a storage space. In a minimalist room, a chair or lamp can also add space to a corner.

Linear Cabin
903 sq ft

Johnsen Schmaling Architects

Saint Germain, Wisconsin,
United States

© John J. Macaulay

A narrow gravel road weaves through the forest and opens
into a small clearing; there, the house is a simple bar that acts
as a threshold between the dense forest of the plateau and the
steep cliff of the lake. The cottage is arranged as three boxes
of the same size, separated by gaps and connected by a thin
flat roof. The result is an unpretentious family retreat with a
characteristic long shape and low rise, offering privileged views
over nearby Lake Alma.

013

Using wood textures on the exterior, even on silhouettes that are far removed from small chalets, helps to create a powerful rustic appearance.

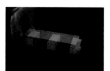

Concept of cabin morphology

Elevation

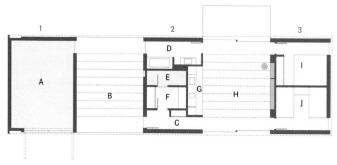

Floor plan

1. Storage box
2. Service box
3. Sleeping box

A. Storage
B. Parking
C. Entrance
D. Bathroom
E. Mechanical room

F. Laundry
G. Kitchen
H. Living/Dining room
I. Master bedroom
J. Bedroom

The three boxes that make up the chalet have different functions: storage, service, and bedroom. The gaps are also different: the closed one accommodates the living room while the open one serves as a carport.

014

Straight lines are essential in small houses, as they help to increase the feeling of space. However, the use of round tables, which occupy less space, is an exception to this rule.

015

Bunk beds often make a room feel smaller. However, if you choose your item well not only does it mean you can have one bed above the other, it can also provide useful storage space.

House Zilvar

1,142 sq ft

Gabriela Kapralova

Lodin, Czech Republic

© Petra Hajská, Gabriela
Kapralova, Veronika Nehasilova

"Every part of this house, both inside and out, radically
changes in appearance with the natural light, allowing the
inhabitant to feel as though they are exploring inside a
canyon." This is the experience that Gabriela Kapralova aims
to communicate in her work, while also meeting the owner's
desire for an open-plan, energy-efficient wooden house, which
favors the proximity of its three family members as much as the
contact with its natural environment.

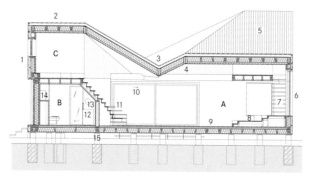

Section

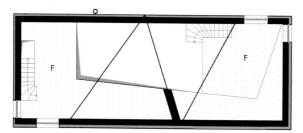

Second floor plan

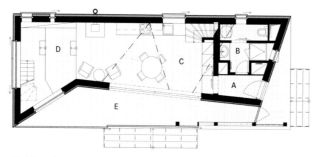

First floor plan

A. Lounge, kitchen and dining area
B. Bathroom
C. Open bedroom galleries

1. 2 by 4 KVH larch timber construction/diffusion
   —open wall assembly/the façade wood cladding
   uses a "burn and stain" technique, for longer-
   lasting life
2. Roof construction—the larch timber-framed
   structure/hydro insulation is hidden under the
   roof wood cladding
3. Roof valley heated when necessary
4. Supporting roof structure—ULTRALAM beam
5. The cladding goes all the way to roof level and
   forms a cover for the roof waterproofing sheet
6. Windows are designed with wood (inside) and
   aluminium (outside) frames and insulated triple
   glazing
7. Subtle stain industrial staircase in front of a
   large window enables view to the close oak tree
8. Podium with storage area
9. Larch timber strip flooring
10. Sliding glass doors with high-performance low-E
    coated glass/windows are designed with wood
    (inside) and aluminum (outside) frames and
    insulated triple glazing
11. Plywood boxes staircase with a storage area
12. Storage water heater
13. Recover unit
14. Water treatment
15. Circular monolithic concrete pillars

A. Entrance hall
B. Bathroom
C. Living space
D. Platform
E. Terrace
F. Gallery/Bedroom

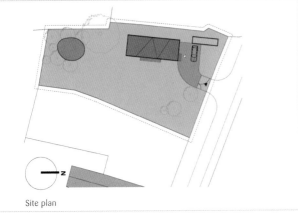

Site plan

The façade, roof, and interior of the house are clad in larch planks; however, the paneling on the exterior uses the "burn and stain" technique, which prolongs the life of the wood.

Thanks to the lightness of their design, metal staircases are practical and aesthetically pleasing, besides saving space and making a room feel larger.

Furniture in small spaces needs to be functional, not just occupy a place. It is also best to have sufficient storage space, preferably with shelves or glass doors.

The main living room, with its large-format glazing, captures the sun in winter. In summer, the large sliding wooden shutters provide protection against the heat.

Sketch

This temporary tiny house has been placed on the site on which the couple have chosen to construct their future home. It provides them with the opportunity to experience life in direct contact with nature, surrounded by the bare essentials they need to live.

How long it will remain will depend on how long it takes to build the main house. In the meantime, it doubles as a workshop, offering the technical advantages needed for ease and speed of construction, as well as the knowledge that the space is being used correctly.

The Shelter
129 sq ft

Castroferro Arquitectos

Vigo, Spain

© Ángel Tourón

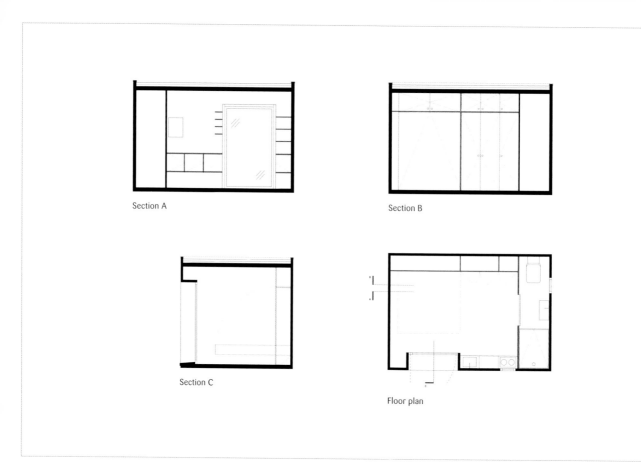

Section A

Section B

Section C

Floor plan

018

In small spaces, installing a shower instead of a bath is practically a necessity if you want to get the most out of the bathroom area.

As an escape from the traffic, noise, pollution, and other inherent aspects of life in a large city, the owners of this house were looking for a place to spend long periods away from the discomforts of urban life. The site chosen was a stopping point for walkers, cyclists, and horse riders and offered fabulous views over the Cantabrian Sea.

Taking the owners' wishes into account, the final design is a small, comfortable detached house—a picture that frames the views of those who pass through the area.

House JG
807 sq ft

Jorge Palomo Carmona

Villaviciosa, Spain

© Angel Baltanás

019

Using fewer materials both inside and out reduces construction costs without compromising on comfort or design aesthetics.

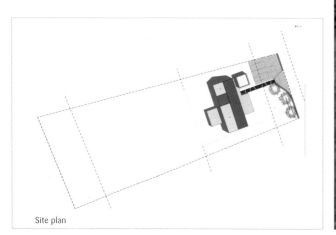

Site plan

West elevation

East elevation

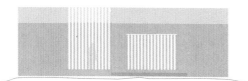

North elevation

South elevation

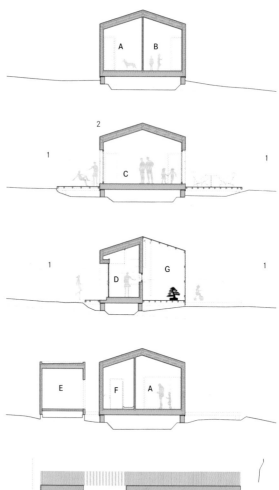

Sections

A. Bedroom 2
B. Bedroom 3
C. Living/Dining room
D. Hall/Kitchen
E. Storage room

F. Bathroom
G. Bedroom 1
H. Terrace

1. Cross ventilation
2. Summer sun

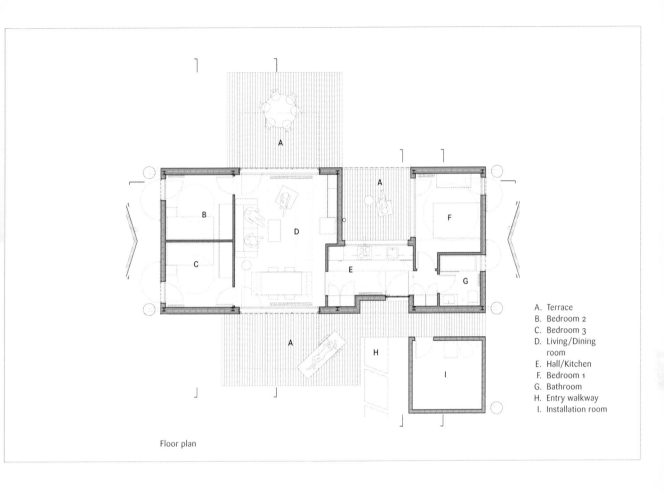

Floor plan

A. Terrace
B. Bedroom 2
C. Bedroom 3
D. Living/Dining room
E. Hall/Kitchen
F. Bedroom 1
G. Bathroom
H. Entry walkway
I. Installation room

A shed connected to the main body of the house can be used both as a laundry and as a dedicated storage area.

This property provides a new and original physical sensation; an interesting spatial experience. The house coexists with its lush natural environment and, through a methodology for configuring unique spaces, gets incorporated within the spectacular natural scenery that surrounds it. Thus, although the outer shape is a simple cube, inside, a series of cubic volumes create a striking vacuum that is inserted between two square floors. This combination results in an experience of order and diversity as a contradiction based on the physical sensation of space.

Villa Kanousan
944 sq ft

Yuusuke Karasawa Architects

Kimitsu, Japan

© Koichi Torimura

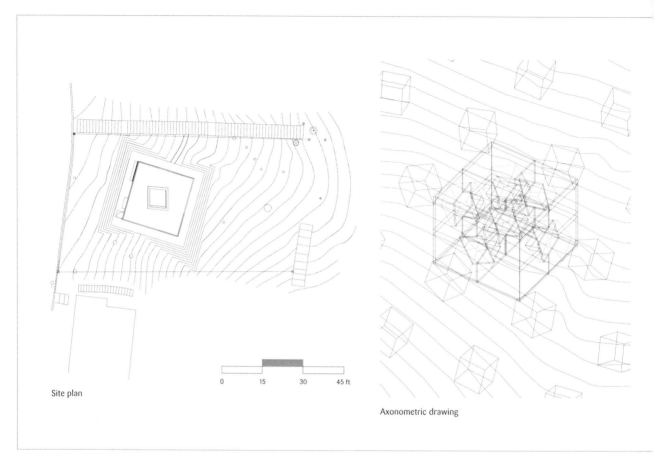

Site plan

0   15   30   45 ft

Axonometric drawing

The rotational angles of the cubic
shapes divide the interior into several
areas and create different spatial
conditions in each of the rooms.

020

In small two-story houses, placing the stairs in the central area influences the interior aesthetics of the building and is a practical way of facilitating access to all the rooms.

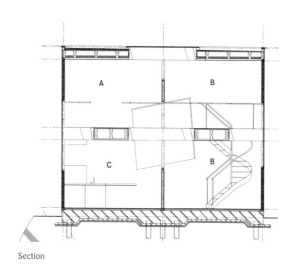

Section

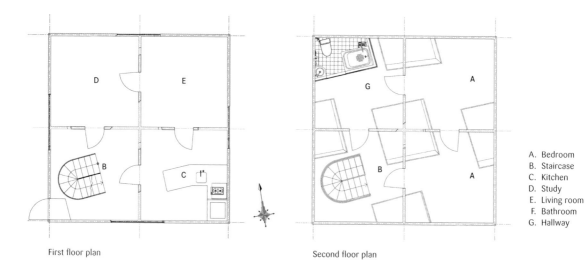

First floor plan

Second floor plan

A. Bedroom
B. Staircase
C. Kitchen
D. Study
E. Living room
F. Bathroom
G. Hallway

021

In tiny houses, rooms such as the kitchen and bathroom, which accommodate most of the technical facilities, need to be treated with special care.

Broken House
431 sq ft

Alejandro Urrutia, Juan Pablo Nazar/UNarquitectura

Curacaví, Chile

© Natalia Vial

The owners already owned a house on the upper section of the site and also wanted a house in the gorge: a simple and independent house that would meet the basic needs of family and friends. A building for visitors, a refuge that would give the impression of being a tree house, from which to enjoy nature by day and gaze at the stars by night.

So as not to interrupt the flow of water in the winter, Alejandro Urrutia and Juan Pablo Nazar's work sits on pillars that also bring the building up to the height of the foliage.

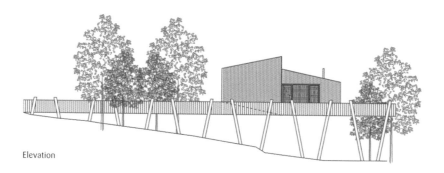

Elevation

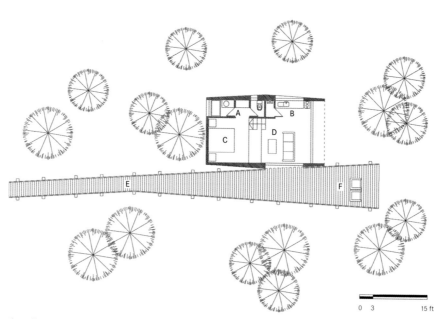

Floor plan

0 3   15 ft

A. Bathroom   D. Living room
B. Kitchen   E. Walkway
C. Bedroom   F. Terrace

The black-painted exterior roots the house in the forest. Inside, white is used to enhance the light.

022

Smooth, light-colored carpets are preferable to those with patterns, which draw the eye toward the ground and reduce the feeling of space. If used well, lines can be a good alternative.

023

In continuous spaces without
any vertical partitions to
define different rooms,
using different floor levels is
another way of differentiating
areas within a single space.

Extension vB4
861 sq ft

dmvA

Brecht, Belgium

© Mick Couwenbergh

Seeking a design that matched with the standard building
style of the area, and which also possessed sufficient strength
to coexist with the silhouette of a pyramid in the main structure,
this design project resulted in a floating habitable shape,
a "tunnel" made from a trapezoidal wooden structure.

In this extension to an existing house, the architectural
concept explores a dialogue between old and new, warmth
and openness, glass and wood, all united by materiality and
attention to detail.

024

Building a few inches above the ground can help to circumvent any irregularities on the plot, reduce the environmental impact of the house, and keep it safe from any rise or fall in the water level.

The front and back of the new area are fully glazed, providing views of the garden and pond. A movable partition wall can be used to hide the view to the street.

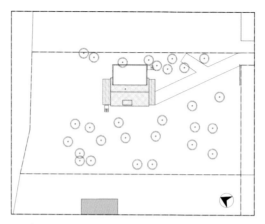

Site plan

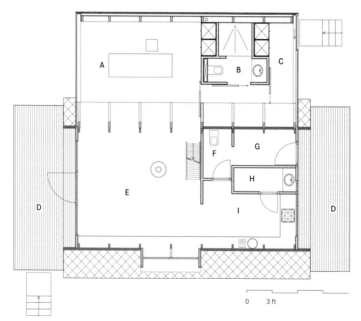

A. Library
B. Bathroom
C. Entrance
D. Terrace
E. Living room
F. Toilet
G. Storage
H. Washroom
I. Kitchen

0   3 ft

Ground floor plan

025

Choosing a piece of furniture in a color that breaks with the general tone of the room provides a focal point and is another way to relieve tight spaces.

026

Careful planning of storage
space helps to do away with
unnecessary furniture. It
relies on the use of just a few,
well-chosen items and in turn
creates more usable space.

027

As well as offering a very adaptable structure, A-frame houses provide highly usable interior space and have relatively low construction costs.

Cloudy House
1,292 sq ft

LASC studio

Copenhagen, Denmark

© Laura Stamer

This architectural project is an extension to a 1930s house that, over time, had become too small to accommodate its young but growing family.

The meeting of the two buildings—the new extension and the existing house—takes place through large picture windows that flood both sides with light and create a subtle connection between the two spaces. The design of the new space retains a sensitivity, collecting and endorsing the features of the old house such as the angles of the ceiling and the special placement of the windows.

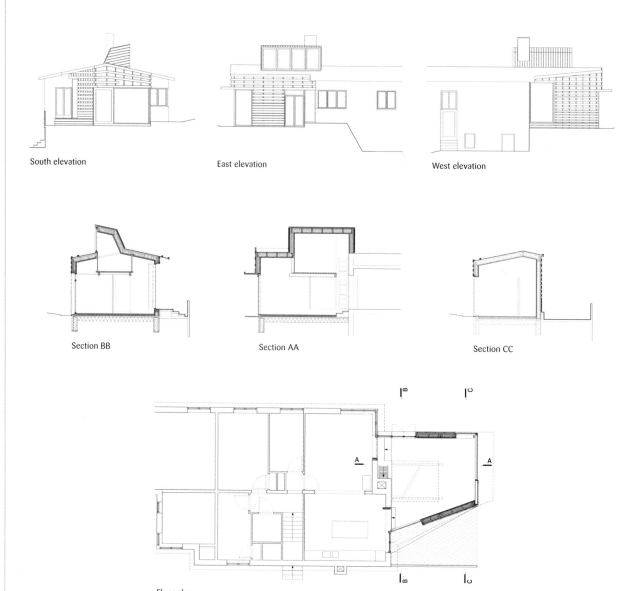

South elevation

East elevation

West elevation

Section BB

Section AA

Section CC

Floor plan

The corrugated wooden façade emphasizes the appearance of the new retractable roof from the existing house. The progressive decrease in density of the slats helps increase the dynamic expression.

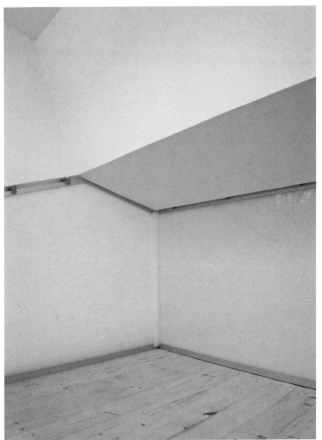

028

In small spaces with high ceilings, installing a mezzanine can create an extra floor, making intelligent use of the full height available.

Treehouse
800 sq ft

Castanes Architects

Puget Sound, Washington,
United States

© Castanes Architects

Immersed in a ravine near the waterfront of the Hood Canal,
this chalet stands on four imposing, robust concrete columns.
A motorized staircase, which is operated as a drawbridge,
provides security when the owners are away or access to
the neighboring quarter mile of coastline when it is down.

The structure respects the different timelines that come together
in the cabin, from the concrete's response to the slow geological
movement of the ground, to the small pieces of wood, which
respond to the short timeline of human occupation.

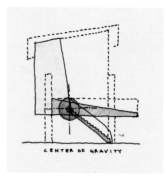
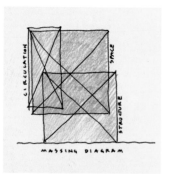
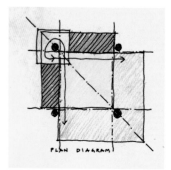
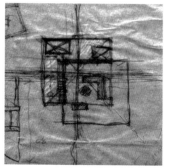

Sketches

029

Large floor-to-ceiling glazing that takes up the bulk of the façade is undoubtedly the best way to increase the sense of space and establish a strong link with the outside.

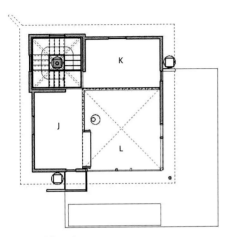

Second floor plan

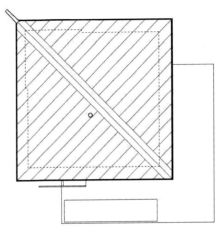

Roof plan

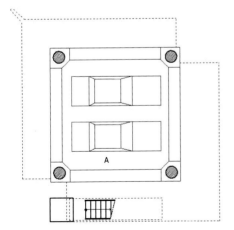

Ground floor plan

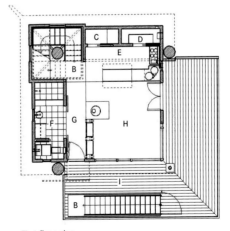

First floor plan

A. Parking
B. Stairs
C. Storage
D. Pantry
E. Kitchen
F. Bathroom
G. Entry
H. Living room
I. Deck
J. Sitting loft
K. Sleeping loft
L. Open to below

030

Installing extendible or retractable furniture in rooms such as the kitchen can customize a space, increasing or decreasing it depending on the needs of the moment.

A galvanized steel ladder works its way around a monolithic concrete column and, on the top floor, provides access to two large rooms, which are used as bedrooms.

"A small house, like a small temple can be a perfect work of art." Following this declaration by Marion Mahony Griffin, benn + penna architecture designed a new building in the form of three separate pavilions, each designated for the different functions of sleeping, living, and working. This configuration is a reflection of the life cycle that is woven into the natural environment in harmonious balance, with the pavilions freely arranged as a natural amphitheatre created from the sandstone of the magnificent Barragorang Valley cliffs.

Southern Highlands
538 sq ft

benn + penna architecture

Burragorang Valley, New South Wales, Australia

© Tom Ferguson Photography

The exterior is entirely clad in fireproof metal sheeting, carefully designed to prevent the space from falling into monotony.

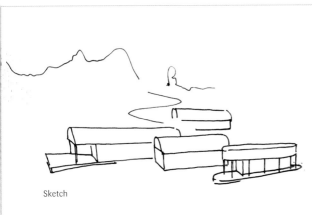

Sketch

031

Keeping spaces clean and tidy and only including furniture that is strictly necessary can significantly enhance the amount of space available.

Holiday House
581 sq ft

Bloem en Lemstra Architecten

Vlieland, the Netherlands

© Chiel de Nooyer

Located on the Dutch island of Vlieland, this small holiday house has an interesting retractable façade that can be opened up fully to the natural environment that surrounds it.

The design was dictated by the area's building regulations and the limited space available. It has a minimal visual impact on the landscape and is simply organized inside: the private areas are on the north side of the building while the communal areas make the most of the views over the southern part of the island.

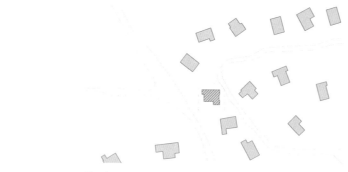

Site plan

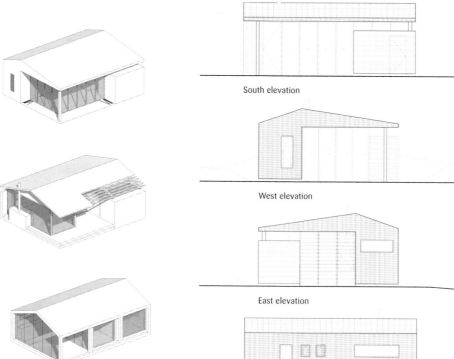

South elevation

West elevation

East elevation

North elevation

Axonometric views of different
house models

032

Using natural wood to coat the exterior gives the house a softer aesthetic than if other types of cladding had been used.

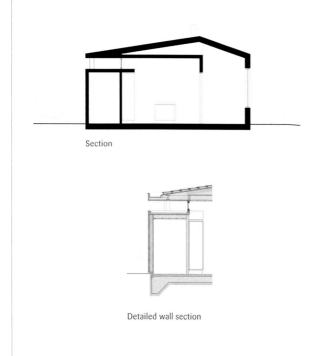

Section

Detailed wall section

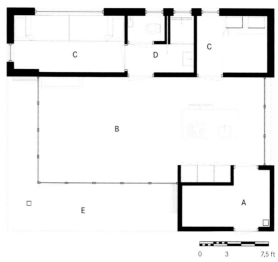

0   3   7,5 ft

Floor plan

A. Entrance   C. Bedroom
B. Living room/   D. Bathroom
   Kitchen   E. Terrace

033

Keeping the floor at the same
height both inside and out
creates the perfect transition
between the two areas as
well as enhancing the feeling
of space.

Located in Brittany, on the northern coast of the Rhuys peninsula, this blackened wood house is a small family holiday home that offers not only beautiful views over the Gulf of Morbihan, but also a rural retreat, with the double option of living both inside and out.

Vertical wooden slats painted black cover the outside of the house and help the building to blend into its environment, while referencing both traditional farm buildings and the salt shops that are found throughout this coastal zone.

Holiday House in Sarzeau
743 sq ft

Raum

Sarzeau, France

© Audrey Cerdan

034

Even in a small house, a green roof acts as a reservoir for rainwater retention, improves heat insulation, and integrates the house in its surrounding landscape.

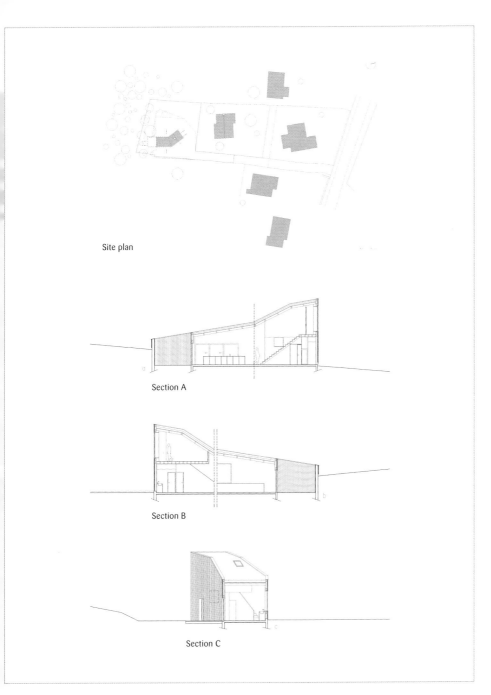

Site plan

Section A

Section B

Section C

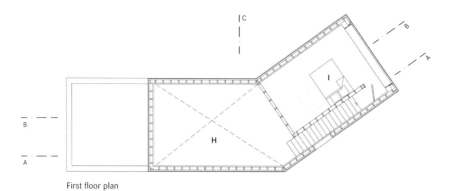

First floor plan

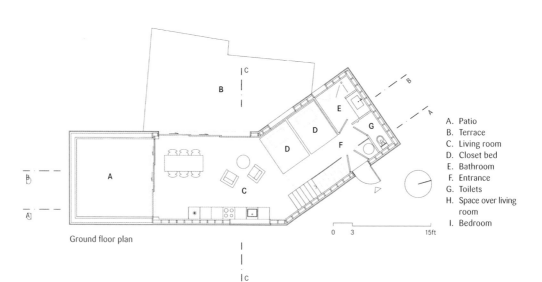

Ground floor plan

A. Patio
B. Terrace
C. Living room
D. Closet bed
E. Bathroom
F. Entrance
G. Toilets
H. Space over living room
I. Bedroom

0   3   15ft

At the other area of the living room a covered patio, with built-in bench and white-painted walls, provides an area that is drenched in sunlight and protected from the breeze.

035

Creating mobile bedrooms
and transferring them outside
creates the sensation of
sleeping in the open air and
also frees up space in the
interior of the house.

Upstairs, the master bedroom opens to the outside through a rectangular window that provides sweeping views of the Gulf of Morbihan and is in constant contact with nature.

Writers' Cottage 2
161 sq ft

**Jarmund/Vigsnæs
AS Arkitekter MNAL**

Oslo, Norway

© Jonas Adolfsen

Located in the large garden, this little annex is designed as an extra part of the main house, while also being quiet enough to work and write.

The architects were also asked to satisfy the owners' desire to make the most of the views that are reminiscent of their land of origin in western Norway, right in the heart of a residential area. The result is a highly satisfactory house that functions as an alternative to a country retreat.

036

In spaces with large glazed areas and plenty of natural illumination, keeping the interior deliberately dark through the use of colors and natural materials creates a nice contrast to the exterior.

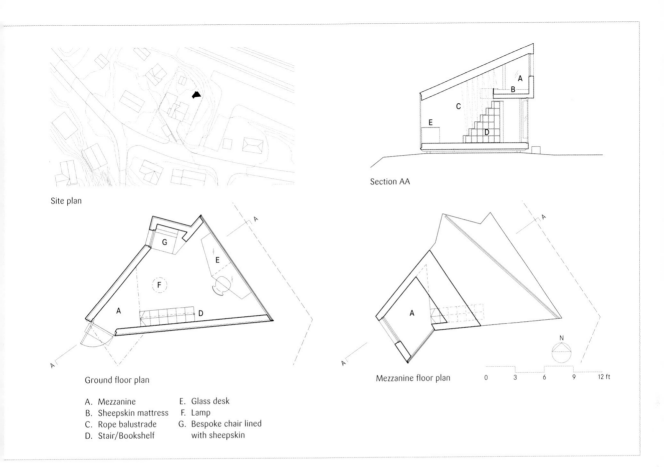

Site plan

Section AA

Ground floor plan

A. Mezzanine
B. Sheepskin mattress
C. Rope balustrade
D. Stair/Bookshelf
E. Glass desk
F. Lamp
G. Bespoke chair lined
   with sheepskin

Mezzanine floor plan

N

0   3   6   9   12 ft

037

Interior stairways take up a lot of space. Installing cupboards, bookcases, and other storage systems underneath can help to make the most of space that would otherwise be wasted.

038

Glass is elegant, delicate, and very versatile. Used in furniture, it creates soft, light designs, which help to increase the feeling of space.

House in Villagarcía
969 sq ft

Nan Arquitectos

Vilagarcía de Arousa, Spain

© Héctor Santos-Diez

"I want to create a cheap, modern house to rent out" was the clear instruction of the owner who built this house.

From this brief description, the best option was to design a low-budget house that could meet the demands of a transient user. To achieve this, he opted for simplicity of forms, circulations, distribution, use, and construction. If modern is defined as "what belongs to the time of the speaker," it was imperative that a current home delivered simplicity, austerity, efficiency, and architectural quality.

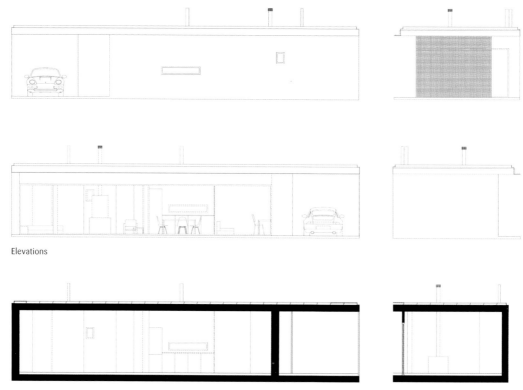

Elevations

Sections

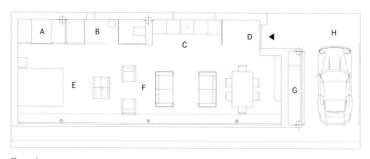

Floor plan

A. Dressing room
B. Bathroom
C. Kitchen
D. Entrance hall
E. Bedroom
F. Living/Dining room
G. Laundry
H. Garage

A big slab of concrete provides the perfect solution for the roof. It floats over the south façade and protects the long picture window from the summer sunshine.

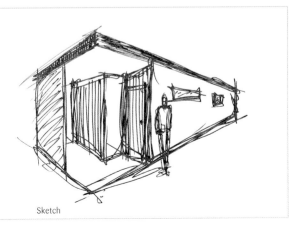

Sketch

039

Directing lights at the ceiling and walls is an intelligent way of increasing the feeling of height in homes with low ceilings.

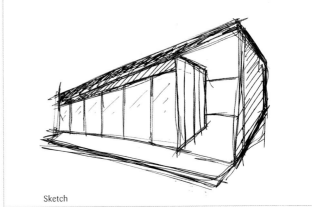

Sketch

040

Choosing curtains in the same color as the wall increases the feeling of space. If they are also translucent, they will not inhibit the interior light and will help to maintain a link with the exterior.

041

Installing a wall-mounted reading lamp in the bedroom frees up space on the bedside table, which can be used for other things that are equally necessary.

042

Using curtains and blinds as mobile walls saves space and enables the elegant, simple, and quick separation of different areas or uses within a single room.

Guest House Renovation
700 sq ft

Pablo Serrano Elorduy

Barcelona, Spain

© dom arquitectura

Since the existing home could not be changed, work was limited to the guesthouse. First, the construction was rehabilitated with the addition of a contemporary insulated and waterproofed roof, then the façades and interior space were addressed.

The main idea was that the interior space should be open to the outside in order to enjoy the large garden and its views. The rattan pergola, an extension of the roof, lengthens the terrace area: now visitors can enjoy direct contact with the garden, nature, and orchard.

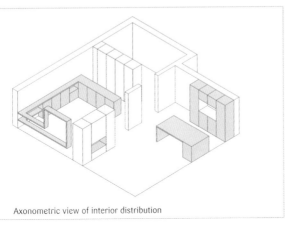

Axonometric view of interior distribution

043

Large overhangs, pergolas, or the installation of large umbrellas, parasols, or awnings provides the ability to enjoy the outdoors while increasing the amount of living space available.

The kitchen furniture, fireside furniture,
and wardrobes, which maintain the
same modulation, are distributed in
an orderly fashion within the space.

044

Side tables are not very appropriate for use in small spaces. However, if you do want one you could opt for a nest of tables—which stores several tables in the space of one—or movable tables.

045

If the nature of a window allows for it, installing a window seat provides better use of space without necessarily reducing the amount of natural light available.

The starting point for this work by Alexander Nägele was a superb plot 750 feet long and slightly more than thirty feet wide with views of the Alps, plus the owner's desire to create a simple, small-scale home.

Legal restrictions and budget helped to determine the structure of the building. The design is environmentally friendly and manages to emphasize the beautiful views of its surroundings—high trees to the north and extensive views toward the Illertal and the Allgau Alps to the south—as an experience that is always present in the house.

Haus Sunoko
1,141 sq ft

**Alexander Nägele/
SoHo Architektur**

Memmingen, Germany

© Rainer Retzlaff,
Niedersonthofen

There are innumerable options when it comes to cladding the façade, from the most traditional to sheets of PMMA (polymethylmethacrylate), which create interesting and eye-catching light effects.

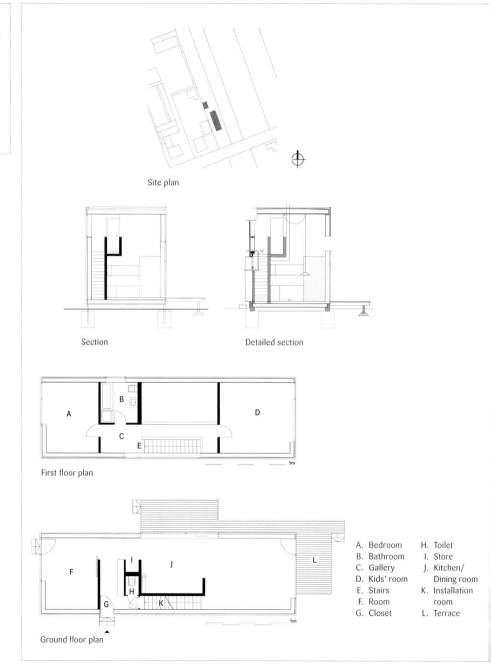

Site plan

Section

Detailed section

First floor plan

Ground floor plan

A. Bedroom
B. Bathroom
C. Gallery
D. Kids' room
E. Stairs
F. Room
G. Closet
H. Toilet
I. Store
J. Kitchen/ Dining room
K. Installation room
L. Terrace

If you must have corridors in
small spaces, it is essential to
keep them clean and free of
obstacles. The walls, however,
can be used to install extra
storage space.

Perched on a sand dune just thirty minutes from Dunedin and surrounded by a multitude of huts built by the fishermen of the area, this Regan Johnston design has elevated the traditional "bach"—the small and modest beach house typical of New Zealand—to a new architectural level.

The natural materials that are used in its construction, together with its discreet pitched roof, are honest, simple, and robust, and provide the house with a rawness that makes it very attractive. Now the "bach" is both stimulating and restful—an inspiring space in which to live.

Taieri Mouth House
969 sq ft

Mason & Wales Architects

Taieri Mouth, New Zealand

© Ewem Livingstone

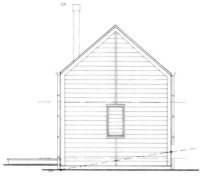

West elevation

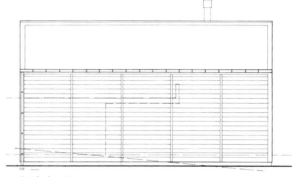

North elevation

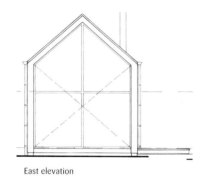

East elevation

South elevation

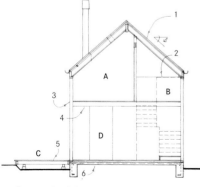

Cross section A-A

A. Dress room
B. Mezzanine
C. Deck
D. Lobby

1. Selected Colorsteel roofing on selected roofing underlay on H1.2 treated ex 75 x 50 purlins @ 900 max crs on H1.2 Ex 150 x 50 rafters @ 900 max crs
2. Stair balustrade shown dashed
3. 190 x 18.5mm Cedar bevel back weatherboards on building paper on H12 ex 150 x 50 timber framing

4. Ex 150 x 25 Rimu flooring on ex 200 x 50 dressing grade Pinus Radiata joists @ 400 crs
5. Ex 150 hardwood decking on H3.2 Ex 150 x 50 joists @ 450 crs on H 3.2 ex 100 x 100 timber bearers @ 1.600 crs on H5 125 x 125 timber piles @ 1.200 crs
6. Ex 150 x 25 Rimu flooring on H3.1 ex 100 x 50 timber battens @ 450 max crs on 100mm concrete slab reinforced with D147 mesh, 30mm cover, lap mesh edges 300mm. Pour slab and footing on 0.25mm polythene D.P.M. over 25mm compacted sand blinding and compacted metal as required (150mm min.)

048

Thanks to its load-bearing capabilities, steel is ideal for use in structures that need to support the weight of large glazed walls, while being light enough not to obstruct the view.

The interior is finished simply in plywood panels. The exterior is clad in cedar wood, with the ends of the planks aligned and covered with decorative vertical pieces for a modern look.

049

Using an open-plan structure means that the house can grow and adapt to the changing needs of its inhabitants and future generations.

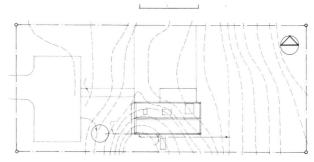

Site plan

1. Garden
2. Connect to wastewater system
3. Adjacent residence
4. Lawn
5. Deck
6. House
7. Gully trap
8. Connect stormwater to rainwater tank
9. Landscape path/Stairs
10. 20000 L Rainwater tank. Set at forecourt level
11. Gravel forecourt
12. Driveway

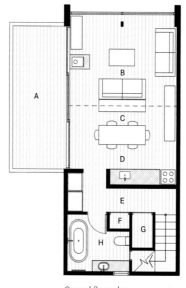

Ground floor plan

Mezzanine floor plan

A. Deck
B. Living room
C. Dining room
D. Kitchen
E. Gallery
F. Store
G. Laundry
H. Bathroom
I. Open to below
J. Skylight
K. Mezzanine bedroom
L. Bedroom
M. Stairs

050

Minimizing clutter in rooms or
open spaces and using hidden
storage areas is a great way
of gaining high-quality space.

The mountain where the chalet sits is a natural treasure, an amazing setting that anyone could fall in love with at first sight.

However, the chalet stands out not just for its location but because it has been built with the aim of achieving design and construction in a single act, creating the same level of freedom as a snowboarder experiences when cutting through powder, making the process an adventure rather than being linked to any type of predetermined action. This is a very special project for Scott and Scott Architects as they designed and built it for themselves.

Alpine Cabin
1,076 sq ft

Scott & Scott Architects

Port Hardy, British Columbia, Canada

© Scott & Scott Architects

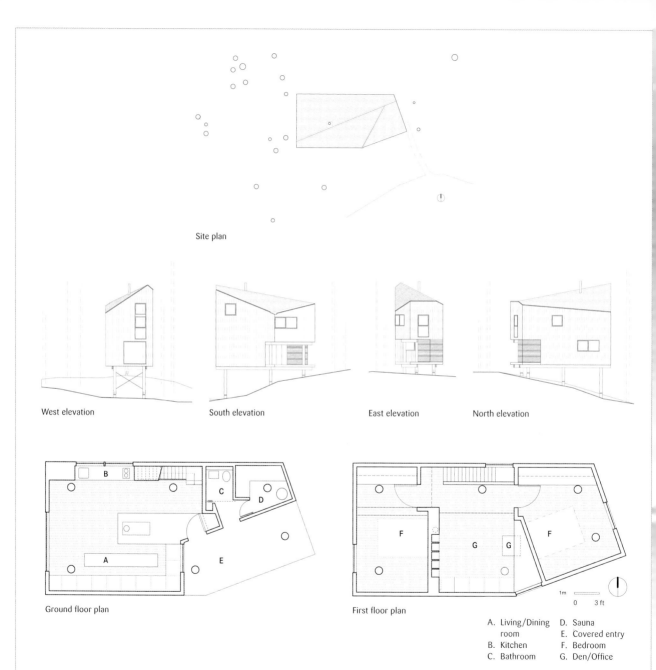

Site plan

West elevation

South elevation

East elevation

North elevation

Ground floor plan

First floor plan

1m
0   3 ft

A. Living/Dining   D. Sauna
   room   E. Covered entry
B. Kitchen   F. Bedroom
C. Bathroom   G. Den/Office

051

A long bench attached to the wall, combined with a chair or rocker, provides adequate seating while using up the minimum possible space.

The chalet has no electricity and is heated by a wood-burning stove. Water is collected directly from a local source and is carried into the home.

052

Using a bed with a storage
base provides plenty of out-
of-sight storage in an area
that would otherwise
be totally wasted.

G House
1,076 sq ft

Lode Architecture

Normandy, France

© Daniel Moulinet

Situated near the Seine estuary, between forests and orchards, this weekend retreat appears suddenly as a dark silhouette against a bright green background.

The house is a simple monochrome structure with a completely smooth façade and sharp edges. The slate cladding reflects the light and reacts to the changing Normandy skies, enabling the building to completely mimic the surrounding landscape. This original house definitely calls to mind the façades of the buildings surrounding the Port of Honfleur.

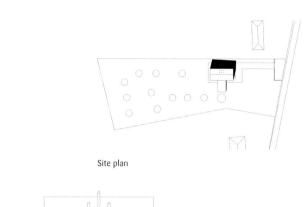

Site plan

North elevation

East elevation

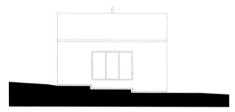

South elevation

West elevation

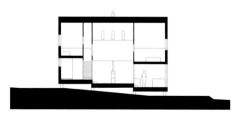

Long section AA'

Cross section EE'

0 3 6   15   30 ft

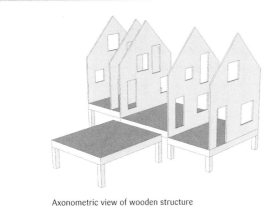

Axonometric view of wooden structure

053

In holiday homes that are used sporadically, environmental decisions prevail: the intelligent use of architecture and passive devices enables great energy efficiency without compromising the comfort of the occupants.

054

As they have a low thermal mass, using a wooden structure for a weekend house enables it to be heated more quickly, for short periods of time with the use of nothing more than a wood-burning fireplace.

The entire structure of the house is made of solid wood panels, completely covering its forty-foot length. The load-bearing walls are made in two pieces with a join in the middle.

First floor plan

Second floor plan

A. Master bedroom
B. Master bathroom
C. Corridor
D. Open to below
E. Bedroom
F. Kitchen/Dining room
G. Living room
H. Bathroom
I. Terrace

0   3   6   15 ft

055

Using wood as a single material in the structure of a building, and as heat insulation, provides excellent levels of insulation and air tightness in a home.

Embedded in the landscape as though it were a barn, this home is a fine example of the homogeneous use of materials—in this case carefully worked raw concrete, which stands out against the green of the meadow and the white of the snow. Its ash-gray color contrasts with the heavy oak front door, while the anthracite railing merges with the branches of the surrounding forest.

Semantically, the expression of the tower creates in the mind the idea of fortified structures and abstract computer figures, so that the tower seems both familiar and strange at the same time.

Mountain Cabin
1,104 sq ft

Marte.Marte.Architekten

Laterns, Austria

© Marc Lins Photography

At the entrance level the structure, with its two corner columns, offers a view right through the bu ilding to a panoramic vista of the landscape.

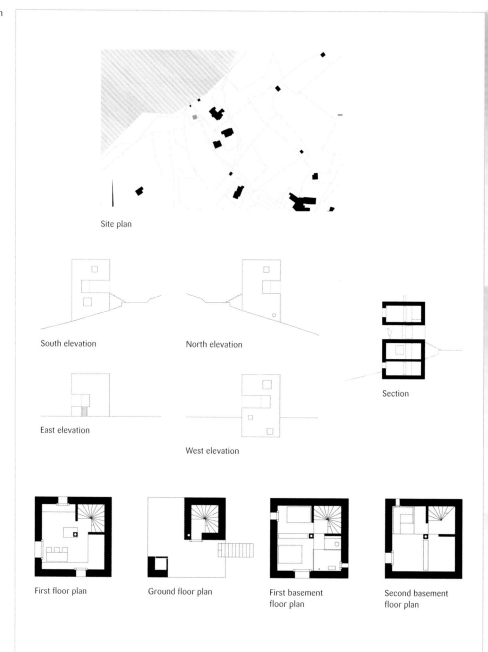

Site plan

South elevation

North elevation

East elevation

West elevation

Section

First floor plan

Ground floor plan

First basement floor plan

Second basement floor plan

056

Using concrete in rural homes gives a feeling of security and robustness to the building, and even more so when balanced in combination with other materials such as wood and glass.

057

Combining two different materials inside the house, such as natural wood and concrete for the furniture, finishes, and fixtures, creates a greater sense of space.

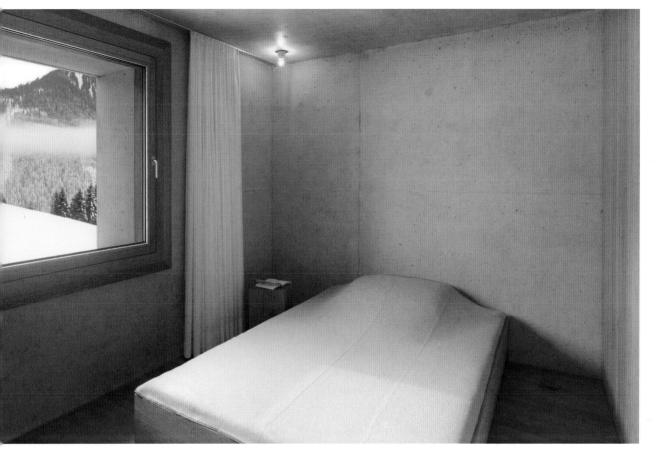

058

An austere and minimalist aesthetic, using as little furniture as possible, is usually the best way to get the most out of a space.

Waterside

Situated between land and sea, this house is a window through which to gaze. The large openings toward Sagami Bay on the one side and toward Mount Fuji and Enoshima on the other facilitate the view when the owner is out, and avoid creating the visual barrier of a beachfront house.

Located on a plot of just ten by twenty-six feet, the house is distributed automatically over three floors. The ground floor, as demanded by the cyclical tides, comprises the pillars on which the main body of the house rests.

Window House
344 sq ft

Yasutaka Yoshimura Architects

Miura, Japan

© Yasutaka Yoshimura

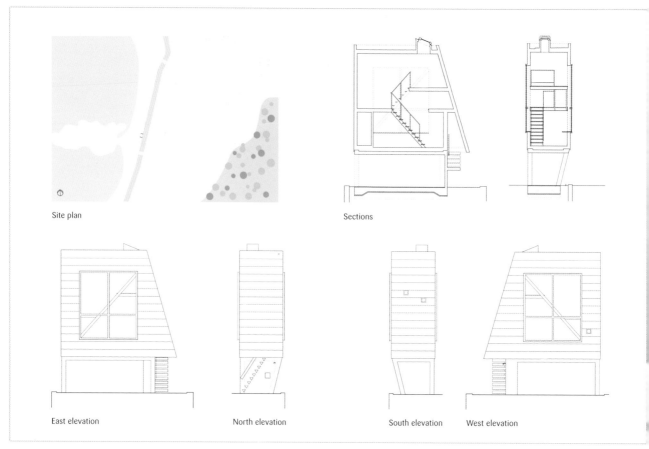

Site plan

Sections

East elevation

North elevation

South elevation

West elevation

The compact design of the interior layout makes the most of the reduced footprint by staggering the various floor levels. This design solution enhances the verticality of the space, offering interesting visual connection between the different levels.

In homes of more than one story, where the inclusion of stairs is essential, it is important to design them carefully so as to make the most of the space available.

When building on a reduced-size plot, one way of improving the house's internal organization, as well as increasing space, is to build upwards.

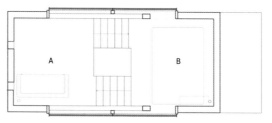

Third floor plan

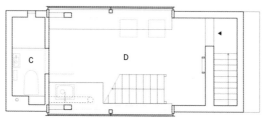

Second floor plan

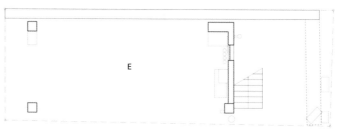

First floor plan

A. Living room
B. Bedroom
C. Bathroom
D. Kitchen
E. Porch

061

Using large windows in tiny homes provides plenty of natural light inside, helping to increase the feeling of spaciousness.

D House
1,033 sq ft

Panorama + WMR Arquitectos

Matanzas, Chile

© Cristobal Valdés

Perched on top of a cliff, about 213 feet above sea level, this house, for a couple and their son, is structured around the creation of two levels within an orthogonal prism of twenty-seven by twenty-seven feet.

The building's main structure is intersected by another interior, on the second floor, which is rotated by 45 degrees so as to generate double heights where it meets the spaces of the first floor. This organization results in three well-defined sections that are orientated toward the panoramic views of the surrounding landscape—the island, the beach, and the forest.

Clad in white wooden panels, the house
boasts different-sized terraces that
are protected from the wind and offer
stunning panoramic views over the sea
in different orientations.

Site plan

062

A studied analysis of the available space can create the opportunity to include terraces in small houses, providing relief to the inner space and enhancing the home's link with its external environment.

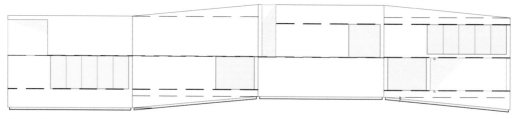

Unfolded façade

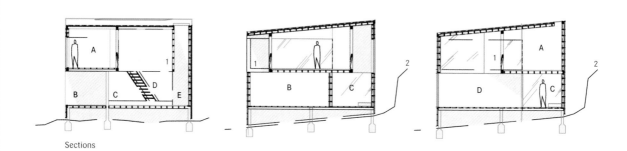

Sections

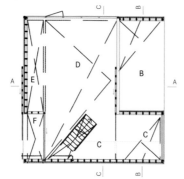

First floor plan

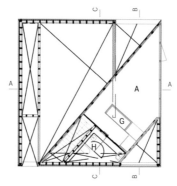

Second floor plan

A.   Master bedroom
B. Terrace
C. Platform
D. Living/Dining room
E. Kitchen
F. Entrance
G. Closet
H. Bathroom

1. Diagonal wall
2. Natural ground level

063

The configuration of the common areas—kitchen, dining room, and living room —as continuous spaces is a natural and easy way to generate both real space and a feeling of spaciousness.

Generated as a second floor, the interior
shape is accessible by a simple wooden
staircase and hosts the master bedroom
and a bathroom.

Seaside Single House
969 sq ft

Modostudio

Monte Argentario National
Park, Italy

© Modostudio

Situated on top of a hill in the Monte Argentario National Park,
this house enjoys incredible views of the sea and the islands of
the Tuscan coast. Modostudio's design has transformed an old
agricultural warehouse into a home, which has been completely
reconstructed using stone salvaged from the original building.

The modifications that have been made to the new building
result in a beautiful combination of the traditional aesthetics
of a country house and a modern home that maximizes the
advantages of its privileged natural setting.

Site plan

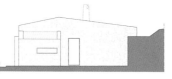

West elevation

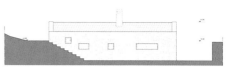

North elevation

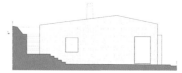

East elevation

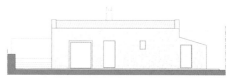

South elevation

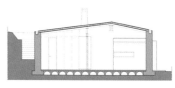

Section A-A

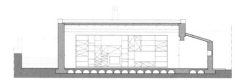

Section B-B

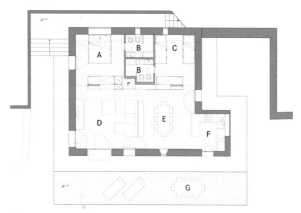

Floor plan

A. Master bedroom E. Dining room
B. Bathroom F. Kitchen
C. Bedroom G. Terrace
D. Living room

3D floor plan

The special roof system is a contemporary reconstruction of the local tradition. It is made from terra-cotta tiles, which are traditionally used in the area.

064

In confined spaces, the choice of furniture is not just a cosmetic question, or a way of obtaining large storage capacity, but can also contribute to sound insulation between rooms.

065

For vacation houses that are located in favorable climates, adding a small lean-to to accommodate the kitchen and a patio on which to dine out of doors creates a strong relationship between inside and out.

Situated on the shore of a lake in northern Bohemia, this project by FAM Architekti replaces an old cottage, maintaining a respect for the unique natural character of the place and following the design of the original building. The objective was to create a year-round refuge for sailing enthusiasts, with minimal topology and maximum visual connection with the lake and the pine forest that surround it. Thus, in addition to careful internal space planning, it encourages the relationship between the lake and its banks as a focal point, represented by the mooring pier as the main point of access.

Lake Cabin
457 sq ft

FAM Architekti,
Feilden + Mawson Prague

Doksy, Czech Republic

© Tomas Balej

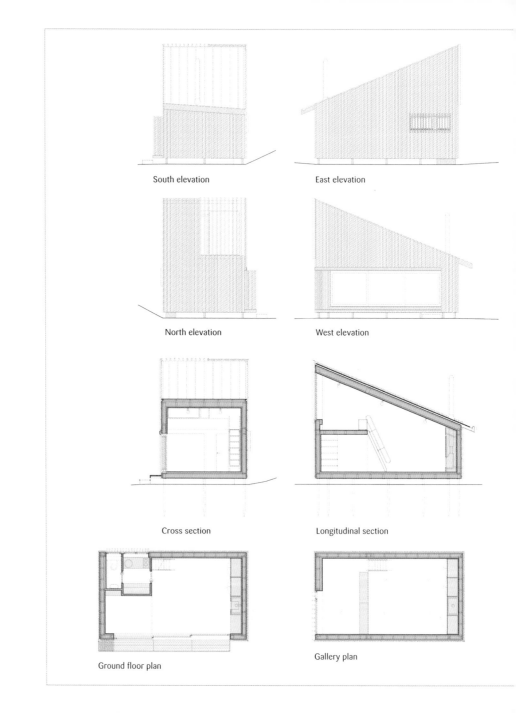

South elevation

East elevation

North elevation

West elevation

Cross section

Longitudinal section

Ground floor plan

Gallery plan

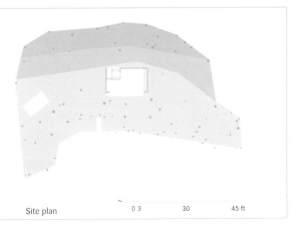

Site plan

0 3   30   45 ft

066

The house's external
appearance—its silhouette,
choice of materials, and
colors—is crucial in order that
it may reflect its surroundings
and manage to integrate easily.

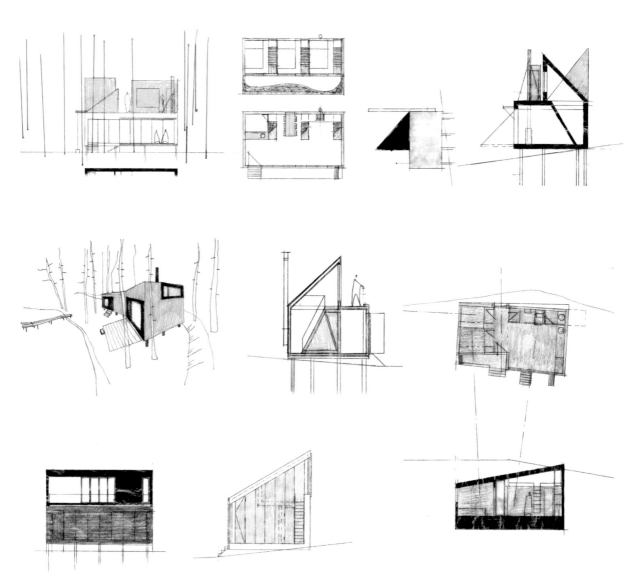

Sketches

At the very top of the chalet is a room for sleeping. Below, a compact black box houses the minimal cooking, bath, and shower facilities.

067

For chalets and holiday homes that remain closed up for long periods of time, security and protection from the elements are important aspects to bear in mind when it comes to maintenance.

068

Installing a floor that is a similar color to the outer surface not only helps to establish a link with the surrounding environment, but it also helps to enhance the feeling of space.

Cabin Dahl
1,076 sq ft

**Jarmund/Vigsnæs AS
Arkitekter MNAL**

Risør, Norway

© Nils Petter Dale

Located in a heavily windswept peninsula, this cabin structure replaces an old 1950s one. The volumetric composition is dictated both by the original structure, for example in the slope that dominates the site, and the desire to create tranquil nooks that are well protected from the prevailing winds.

As well as bringing the outside appearance of the house closer to the granite stone that dominates the site, the metallic exterior cladding—made of zinc—moves away from the traditional design aesthetic of such cabins, which are usually built of wood.

Site plan

069

Well-designed terraces and
outdoor spaces create spatial
continuity with the interior
and add extra open-air living
spaces, which are protected
from the wind and other
weather elements.

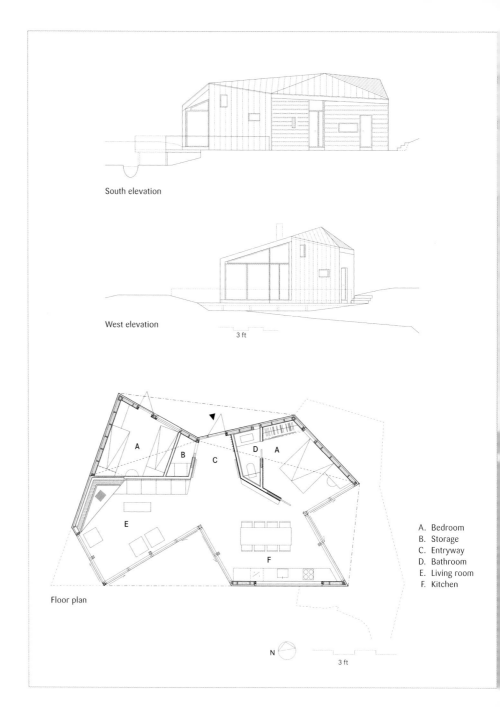

South elevation

West elevation

3 ft

Floor plan

A. Bedroom
B. Storage
C. Entryway
D. Bathroom
E. Living room
F. Kitchen

N

3 ft

Finished with a polished concrete floor, the interior resembles, both in color and in feel, the rocky exterior with its predominance of granite.

Polygon Studio
609 sq ft

Jeffery S. Poss + Workus LLC

Lake George, New York,
United States

© Jeffery S. Poss, FAIA

The owners of this precipitous residential property overlooking
Lake George wanted to create a small studio in which they
could work on their sculptural creations and comfortably put
up their guests, all in a single space. The characteristic final
silhouette of the building absolutely reflects this dual function.

The main challenge was to make an impact using a small space
and budget. Both limitations have certainly been overcome
thanks to this memorable architectural profile.

070

Combining very different
materials such as natural
wood and metal inside and
out can create a strong and
eye-catching contrast between
coldness and warmth.

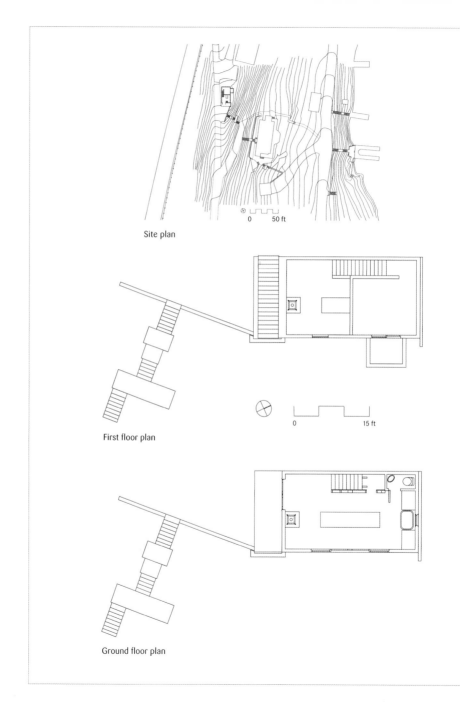

Site plan

0   50 ft

First floor plan

0   15 ft

Ground floor plan

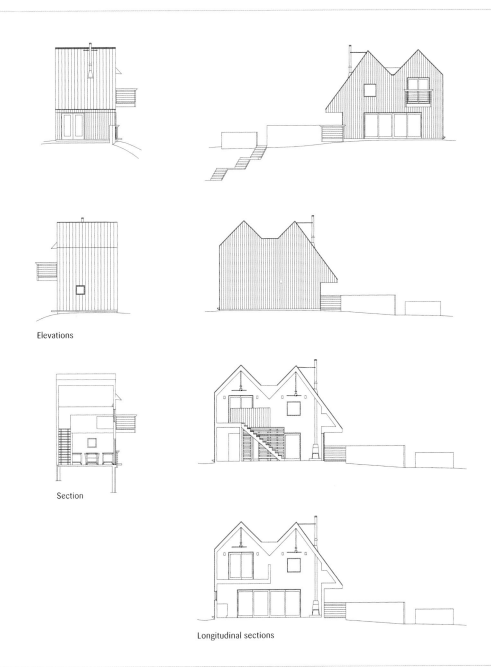

Elevations

Section

Longitudinal sections

071

Using open bookcases with
no doors or closures creates
greater open space and
minimizes visual overload
in confined spaces.

072

Using cedar as the main interior finish not only lends a sense of warmth to all the natural wood, but also provides a characteristic and pleasant aroma.

The typical wooden houses of the Adriatic coast, known as "fishing machines," were the main inspiration behind this beautiful maritime home.

With simplicity as its starting point, the design dispenses with the house's original features to become a real "room in the sea." It remains traditional while taking on a new appearance that embraces new uses. Despite the changes, however, the house's interior retains its profound visual penetration of the sea, the inextricable link between the house and its natural environment.

Trabocco
258 sq ft + 1206 sq ft platform

Studio Zero85

Pescara, Italy

© Sergio Camplone

This 48-square-foot house accommodates the living and sleeping areas within the same space. The remaining space accommodates a kitchen at the rear.

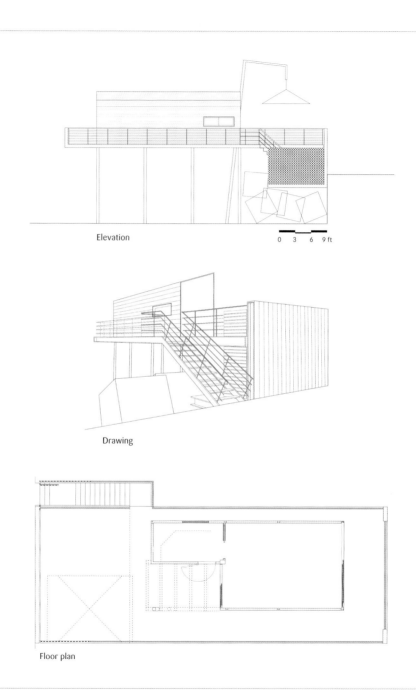

Elevation

0   3   6   9 ft

Drawing

Floor plan

073

A natural environment such
as a maritime setting, with
its demanding environmental
conditions, is not an
impediment to installing
a tiny home.

074

Lines are important. Installing
the flooring in the direction
of the exterior enhances the
feeling of space as it leads the
eye easily from inside to out.

075

When you have outdoor space, patios and terraces are an intelligent way of gaining extra space that is not available inside. They also help to strengthen the ties between the house and its environment.

Urban Environment

Reza Alibadi's vision of creating innovative and affordable designs is realized successfully in the mission to change the face of Toronto. While the construction costs are almost the same as for a standard house, this new home also offers the surprise factor of its design for the neighborhood.

Using low-cost strategies such as buying a plot just twenty feet wide, he is able to keep the budget low and change the perception of custom-made designer houses as being items of luxury.

Shaft House
1,400 sq ft

rzlbd [Reza Aliabadi]
Toronto, Ontario, Canada
© borXu Design

076

Aluminum is ideal for building small houses. It is light and recyclable and has lower production and transport costs than traditional materials such as brick and stone.

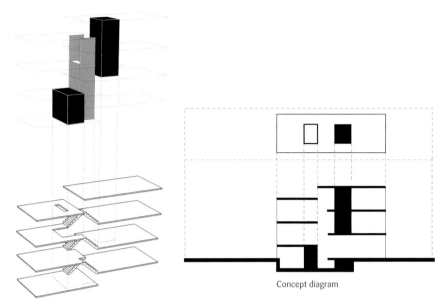

Axonometric diagram

Concept diagram

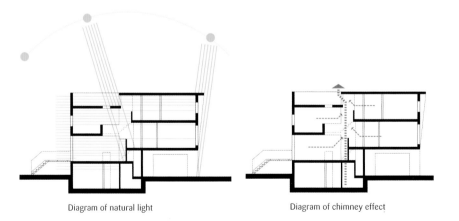

Diagram of natural light

Diagram of chimney effect

The spatial arrangement of the levels overlooking each other creates multi-purpose rooms that can be arranged according to needs of privacy and their relationship with the central axis of the house.

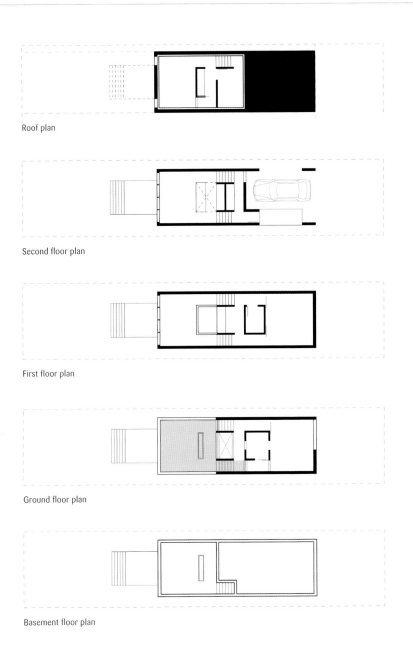

Roof plan

Second floor plan

First floor plan

Ground floor plan

Basement floor plan

077

If you have enough space you can use a kitchen island as a table, making it a comfortable and modern way of gaining space, by eliminating the dining table.

078

The vertical distribution of the rooms around a central axis allows natural light to penetrate the house and affects the perception of the overall size of the spaces.

This house is named after a typical Japanese house built on a very narrow plot, usually no more than fifteen feet wide.

With this home, built on such a plot, the architect indulged his desire to explore how urban life can be developed in compact and efficient spaces. Using a simple, minimalist vertical construction, he succeeded in making use of every square foot of space to create a place in which to live and work.

Eel's Nest
960 sq ft

Anonymous Architects

Los Angeles, California,
United States

© Steve King

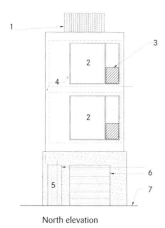

North elevation

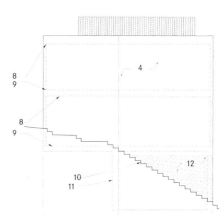

East elevation

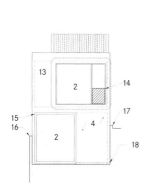

South elevation

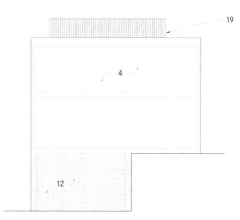

West elevation

1. 42" high guardrail
2. Tempered glass
3. Metal guardrail
4. Stucco fin
5. New side door
6. Existing garage door
7. Sidewalk

8. Finish ceiling height
9. Finish floor height
10. Existing concrete stair
11. Existing concrete retaining wall behind
12. (e) Concrete wall
13. Typical window

14. 42" high metal guardrail
15. Operable stl. frame glass door
16. Top of existing concrete block wall
17. Top of existing retaining wall

18. Weep screed 4" above ground level
19. 42" high guardrail with greater than 75% open area per LABC

079

In a narrow house, configuring the kitchen in a line, with most of the furniture installed on a single wall, is the best solution for making the most of the available space.

Second floor plan/Site plan

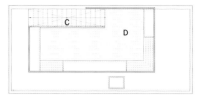

Roof plan

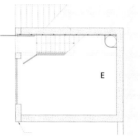

Garage plan

A. Kitchen   E. Garage
B. Yard   F. Bedroom
C. Stairs   G. Bathroom
D. Roof

Third floor plan

In order to give its inhabitants a little more breathing space, a special permit was obtained to enlarge the project. The enlargement of the space was achieved simply by increasing the height.

080

Add a touch of color. As long as there is good lighting, creating a clear contrast between the general light tone of a room by painting a wall in a darker color helps to create a greater sense of space.

The black exterior wall covers the entire cube that is the house. Inside, behind the heavy door, the space becomes bright yellow thanks to the larch plywood cladding.

This house seems to be a different world, a hideout, in which the space is ambiguous and there is no separation between the rooms. An original concept, it allows the space to be used freely. The black cube is home to a free world, one that gets bigger, as though it were an anthill.

Ant-House
713 sq ft

mA-style architects

Shizuoka, Japan

© Kai Nakamura

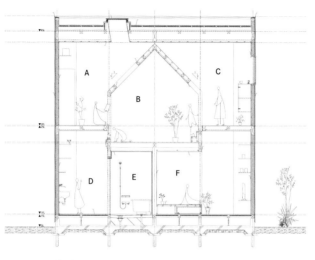

Section

First floor plan

Second floor plan

A. Adult's space   H. Entrance
B. Free space   I. Toilet
C. Child's space   J. Storage
D. Lavatory   K. Kitchen
E. Bathroom   L. Dining room
F. Living room   M. Study room
G. Porch

081

Using stainless steel
appliances and finishes not
only provides a modern and
avant-garde kitchen style,
it also helps to increase the
feeling of space.

082

Aligning rooms such as the kitchen and laundry together with other elements such as the study area or storage shelves can save space and creates a kind of passageway.

Between the first and second floor,
a gable-roofed area creates an empty
space inside. Here, the sunlight and
wind filter through the different
openings in the façade.

"A home that unites community, art, and nature." Emerging from endless conversations between the architects and their clients, this was the principal idea that guided the project.

The result is a village on the outside and a home on the inside—a home that defies logic, since the outside comprises a series of small structures, while inside the spaces and their functions are enlarged. The house is an original combination of small, interconnected individual structures, whose scale and texture prevent them from dominating the environment.

Tower House
2,422 sq ft

Andrew Maynard Architects

Alphington, Victoria, Australia

© Peter Bennett, Tess Kelly

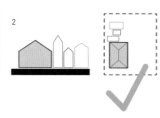

1. **Big and shiny**
   Typically new architectural extensions fail at producing a scale respectful of the original building. Often the large new form dominates the old.
2. **Tall and slender**
   Instead we break down the form by building a cluster of village-like pavilions, which are connected internally as one. The individual forms are tall and slender and reminiscent of the existing hip roof. The play in scale and form work with the old to complement each other.

Silhouette

1. Landscape/decking as objects
2. Landscape integrated

Landscape

Colours

1. Existing garage
2. Clad in "village" aesthetic
3. Adapt existing docile garage to an element that contributes to the site narrative
4. Village of "houses"
   The new form of the garage works with the new extension to form and accentuate the village of "houses" concept

1. The "village" is clad in shingles each with a slightly different tone, giving each "house" a different personality while bounded by form and texture
2. Dr. Who's tardis effect, individual blocks give the perception of small internal spaces; however, internally the houses are connected to form a large free-flowing space. Also the black sophisticated shingles create a clear contrast with the warmth of the internal timber lining.

A. Dark sophisticated shingles externally
B. Warm timber lining internally

A. Hangout space
B. Study

1. Instead of a floor, we can install a netting above the study space, great space to relax and read a book; the netting will also allow light to pass through and filter down the bottom

Study tower

Design strategy passive solar

A. Summer sun
B. Winter sun
C. Awning extended
D. Inside
E. Outside
F. Shared
G. Retractable fabric awning. Optional shading
H. Steel awning. Permanent shading

1. Passive solar gain
Living spaces to the north allow for great passive solar gain to occur in winter, while in summer the steel awnings cut out the harsh sun and reduce heat gain; also a large deciduous tree to the north will provide additional shade for the house and cool down the summer breeze.

2. Extend awning
Retractable fabric awning are installed above the steel awning, which can be extended for additional shade and a larger covered outdoor space.

3. In and out
Clear distinction between external and internal spaces

4. Shared
When the doors are slid away, the interior and exterior are blurred and the house itself will basically become a covered exterior space.

The house is structured as a "village," which is covered with tiles of a slightly different shade, giving each "house" its own personality, and defining it through their shape and texture.

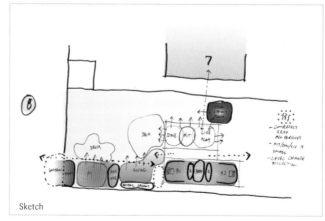

Sketch

Gently submerged in the ground, with the desk almost buried in the garden, the library is a quiet space that invites reflection and contemplation.

083

When it comes to choosing chairs and tables, and indeed furniture in general, straight lines, light forms, and soft feet or supports are ideal for creating a feeling of greater space.

Ground floor plan

084

Installing a grid to provide height separation to spaces is a rare but very original option. It enhances the space and enables natural light to filter unimpeded right into every corner.

085

Distributing the total space into smaller individual spaces with distinct structures and functions is another way of getting the best out of living in confined spaces.

Built for a couple and their young son, this narrow house is located in a densely urbanized area of Osaka. At just eleven feet wide and forty-three feet deep, the size of the plot and the way in which every conceivable space has been used are the most striking features of this house.

Built in the traditional Japanese "bed of eels" style, thanks to its original design it manages to accommodate six distinct levels inside. "Living in this house is like being a bird, swinging from branch to branch."

Kakko House
1,224 sq ft

Yoshihiro Yamamoto | YYAA

Osaka, Japan

© Keishiro Yamada

086

In small houses with two or more floors, careful space planning can create a parking space or storage room on the ground floor.

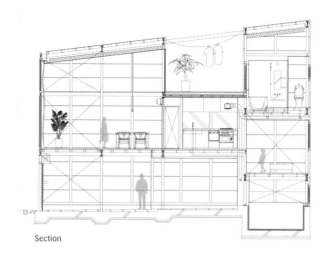

Section

Second floor plan

Roof plan

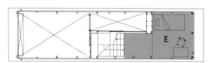

First floor plan

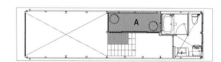

Fourth floor plan

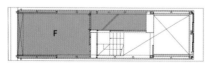

Ground floor plan

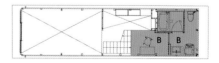

Third floor plan

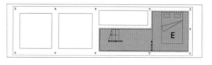

Basement floor plan

A. Terrace
B. Bathroom
C. Living/ Dining room
D. Kitchen
E. Bedroom
F. Garage

The house stands on a large, white-painted visible steel structure and is covered with thin, adiabatic, fire-resistant panels.

087

In the lounge or living room, use comfortable armchairs or three-piece suites instead of large sofas, as they make the most of the space without compromising on comfort.

Painted in white like the walls and the steel structure that supports the building, the metal staircase connects all the levels of the house, spreading natural light throughout the interior.

088

Walls define the space. Using light colors such as white, beige, and gray and light pastel tones is the best way of enhancing the interior space.

089

Having kitchen utensils on display creates a sense of disorder and reduces the feeling of space. It is a good idea to use a cabinet or shelf to store them or use hooks for frying pans and accessories.

It was the unusual layout of the land, fan-shaped and situated near the top of a hill, that caught the attention of the owner and resulted in the subsequent construction of a unique architectural structure. In a newly developed residential area, full of contemporary buildings and devoid of any vestige of traditional urban landscape, the design focused on two main factors: the complete use of the land's shape and location and, at the express request of the owner, the creation of an open interior space without divisions.

House in Muko
1,078 sq ft

Fujiwaramuro Architects

Kyoto, Japan

© Toshiyuki Yano

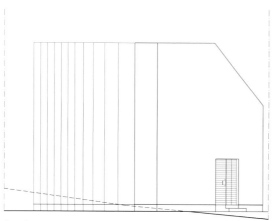

East elevation

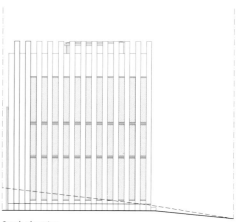

South elevation

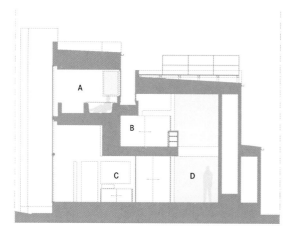

Section X-X

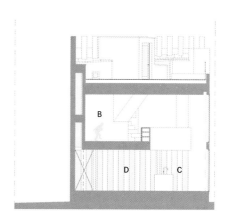

Section Y-Y

A. Bathroom
B. Kids' room
C. Kitchen
D. Living room

090

The absence of adjacent
buildings in urban or
residential areas provides
scope for finding ways of
making the most of the
natural light.

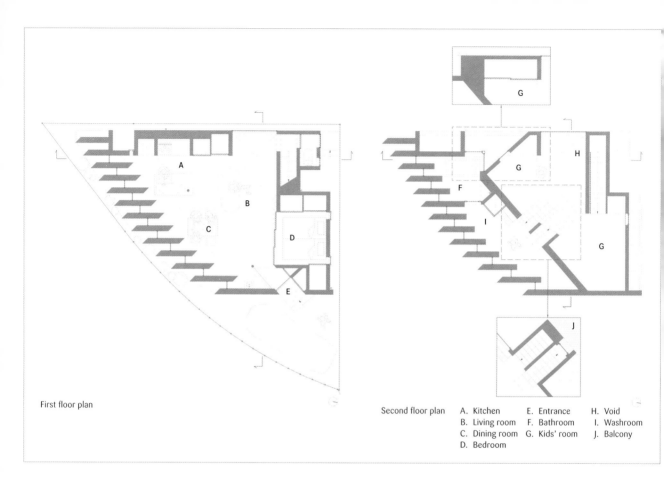

First floor plan

Second floor plan

A. Kitchen E. Entrance H. Void
B. Living room F. Bathroom I. Washroom
C. Dining room G. Kids' room J. Balcony
D. Bedroom

091

Designing interiors in a single space, without divisions between rooms, maximizes the total space available within the home.

The huge strips are the most striking
feature of the façade; they also act as
shutters to regulate the interior light
and block the views from outside in.

Located in Matsudo, a city that has developed as a residential area on the outskirts of Tokyo since the 1960s, this is a house for a young couple and their son. Planned as a reconstruction of the house it once was, it now seeks to become a new landmark in the city, but as a living symbol, not just an imaginative one.

Thus, although the house may be nothing more than a low space beneath a large roof, the loose division of the interior using Y-shaped frames and platforms enables its inhabitants to feel as though they are together while being situated in different spaces.

House H
1,242 sq ft

Hiroyuki Shinozaki, Sota Matsuura, Tatsumi Terado Structural Studio

Matsudo, Japan

© Fumihiko Ikemoto

Site plan

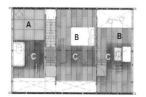

Second floor plan

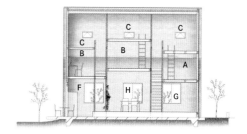

First floor plan

A.	Tatami	E.	Kitchen
B.	Bedroom	F.	Terrace
C.	Loft	G.	Living room
D.	Bathroom	H.	Dining room

Sections

A.	Tatami	E.	Kitchen
B.	Bedroom	F.	Terrace
C.	Loft	G.	Living room
D.	Bathroom	H.	Dining room

092

When designing an interior, focusing the flow line around a space or room helps to ensure that the flow of the residents around their space will be fluid and natural.

The flow line is planned around the kitchen. From here you can see the entire first floor, hear visitors outside, and easily communicate with the children who frequently pass in front.

093

Besides being attractive and easy to operate, sliding doors and walls can free up considerable space thanks to the versatile configuration of the interior.

The preconditions of the land and the very location of the main house combine to perfection in this inspired extension that has created something that was not there before, something that no one expected, even the architects: a reinterpretation, or the offering to its inhabitants of a way of interacting with the environment that was not previously possible.

You could call this a new site, or even a new platform or framework, which gives a different perspective or reinforces the old one.

59 Bellevue Terrace
323 sq ft

Philip Stejskal Architecture

Fremantle, Western Australia, Australia

© Bo Wong

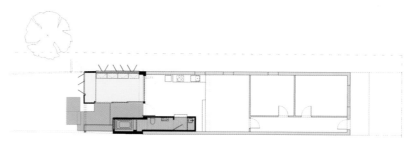

Floor plan of terrace alterations and additions

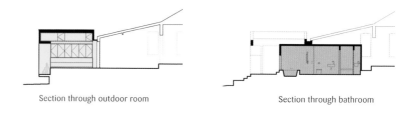

Section through outdoor room

Section through bathroom

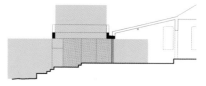

Section through pathway

North elevation

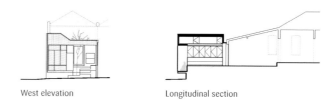

West elevation

Longitudinal section

094

A cleverly designed façade with multiple configuration options for doors and windows enables the residents to adapt the house to changing environmental conditions.

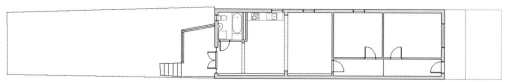

Existing floor plan

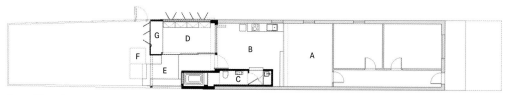

Ground floor plan

A. Existing house
B. Existing kitchen
C. New bathroom
D. New enclosed
   terrace

E. Deck
F. Brick steps
G. Sunken bay
   windows

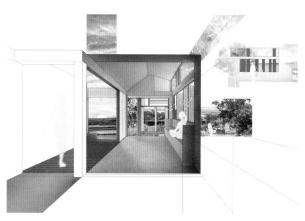

Perspective drawing of new enclosed terrace

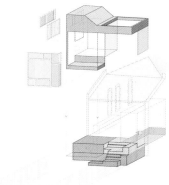

Diagram of terrace alterations and additions

095

In small houses, one of the main objectives is to create spaces that can be configured in different ways and perform multiple functions.

Haringey Brick House
549 sq ft

Satish Jassal Architects

London, United Kingdom

© Paul Riddle

This new two-story house with a single bedroom stands on the plot of an old abandoned garage.

The adjacent Victorian terraces, together with the reduced size of the plot, influenced the final design and foster the predominance of horizontal lines, vertical window proportions, and the use of brick as a cladding on the façade. Thus in a fluid and modern way, the new house establishes a connection with its immediate environment, including the neighboring characteristic Victorian houses.

The materials in this building are very important. Brick, antique brass, and oak are used because they all have an inherent tendency to improve with the passage of time.

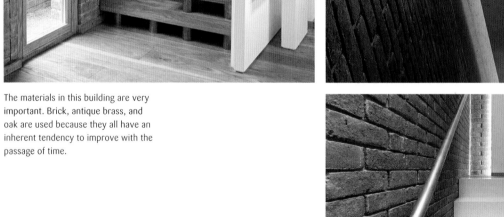

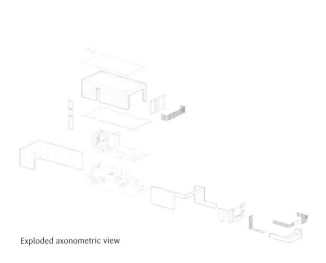

Exploded axonometric view

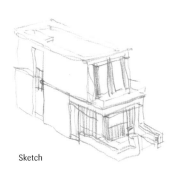

Sketch

Street elevation

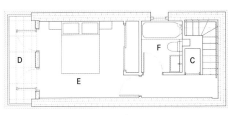

First floor plan

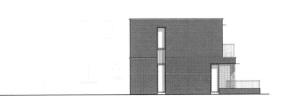

West elevation

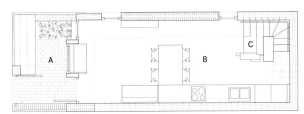

Ground floor plan

A. Terrace
B. Living/Dining room/Kitchen
C. Stairs
D. Balcony
E. Bedroom
F. Bathroom

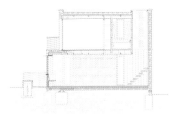

Detailed section

096

Using custom-made furniture, which engages with the spatial characteristics of the house, is another way to make the most of the space, as well as being adaptable to the aesthetic tastes of the owner.

097

Including a kitchen bar is not usually an option in confined spaces. However, if it is reduced to a simple pair of wooden supports and used as a dining table, there is no discernible reduction in space.

098

Mirrors are great when it
comes to enhancing space.
Be they in bedrooms,
bathrooms, or living rooms,
mirrors increase the feeling
of space simply by visually
duplicating it.

Lorraine Studio
1,200 sq ft

Jacobs Chang Architecture

Los Angeles, California,
United States

© Michael Wells

The renovation of this old garage was driven by the
requirements of Los Angeles residential ordinances, which
dictated that the building should have sufficient space to
accommodate two covered parking spaces.

However, the owner's desire to park outside allowed Jacobs
Chang to come up with the idea of reconstructing the building
so that what was once a garage would become an art studio/
pool house on the ground floor and serve various functions
such as studio, games room, or bedroom in the upper floor,
which was also remodeled.

North elevation

South elevation

Cross section

Longitudinal section

The new house stands in the same
location as the original garage built
in 1922; however, its structure is
now larger.

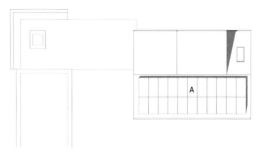

Roof plan

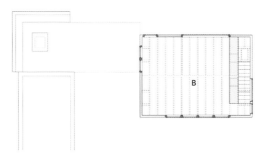

Second floor plan

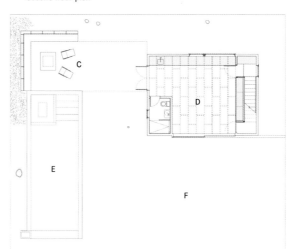

First floor plan

A. Solar array
B. Loft
C. Fire pit
D. Graphic studio
E. Pool
F. Lawn

099

Keep windows and doors open as much as possible. Not only does this establish a strong internal-external link, it also creates the illusion that the room is larger than it is.

100

Open shelves catch the eye, increase the feeling of space, and demand that the inhabitant live in an organized manner, which is essential in small spaces.

Elmwood Cottage
432 sq ft

Turnbull Griffin Haesloop

Berkeley, California,
United States

© David Wakely

This new accessory home is the result of a courtyard
remodeling and renovation, which provides privacy and
protection to both the new home and the main house.

Taking into account the owners' desire to find a new use for
the old garage, the garden is configured with a pitched structure,
thus maximizing the exterior views without compromising on
privacy. This is a design that succeeds in meeting its owners'
wishes and adding to the beauty of the whole.

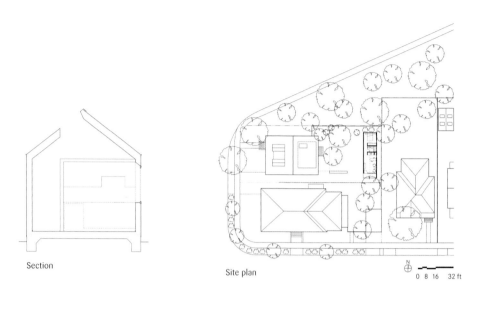

Section

Site plan

N

0 8 16   32 ft

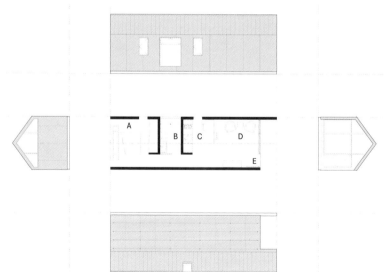

A

B   C   D

E

Floor plan and elevations

A. Bedroom
B. Bathroom
C. Kitchen
D. Dining/
   Living room
E. Entrance

101

Small pictures on large walls can have the effect of shrinking a space. A large picture, such as a landscape, can have the opposite effect and help to make the space feel larger.

102

Besides changing the apparent size of a space, skylights have the effect of subtly changing the interior with the passing of the seasons and during the course of the day.

103

Designing a small central block that houses the bathroom, kitchen, and a storage area creates separation between the bedroom and the living room.

Naoko Horibe's client asked him to combine two completely opposite concepts when designing this house. In one single structure, the exterior of the house was to resemble a sports car with no visual interruptions, while the interior was to be made entirely of natural wood. The specially chosen name of the project succeeds in reflecting the dual role that the house's design follows, paying homage to Italian sports cars in the exterior and at the same time offering a wooden interior.

Arboleda
804 sq ft

Naoko Horibe

Anan, Japan

© Kaori Ichikawa

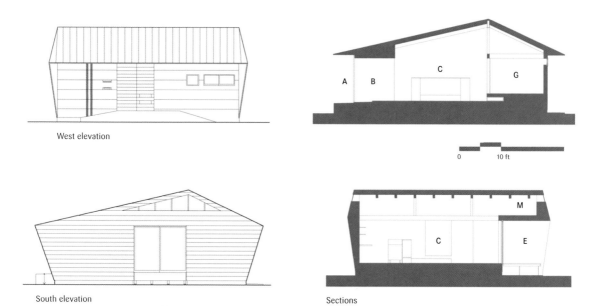

West elevation

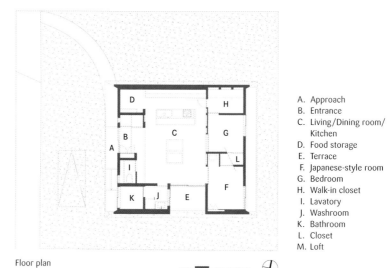

South elevation

Sections

0   10 ft

Floor plan

0 3 6   15 ft

A. Approach
B. Entrance
C. Living/Dining room/
   Kitchen
D. Food storage
E. Terrace
F. Japanese-style room
G. Bedroom
H. Walk-in closet
I. Lavatory
J. Washroom
K. Bathroom
L. Closet
M. Loft

Through the triangular window that crowns the view is a small, open space that has been specifically designed for hosting wedding ceremonies.

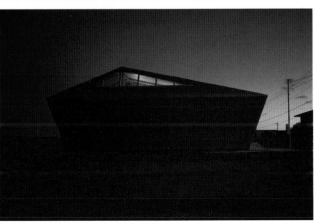

104

Doing away with corridors in the design of a home not only frees up space, it can also provide easy access to all the rooms from a central area.

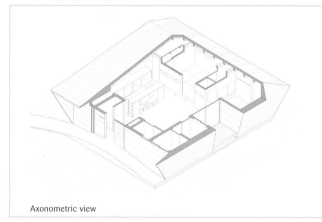

Axonometric view

105

By its very nature, natural wood is a very versatile material for use in constructing houses of any shape or size. It also brings warmth and character to the interior design.

It is the size of this property that first captures our attention—it is just under eight feet wide by thirty-six feet deep. The plot is typically known as a "bed of eels," where one can touch the walls on both sides because of the extreme proximity of the buildings. Most of the space is reserved so as to psychologically create the greatest possible feeling of space for the inhabitant. The house has been conceived as "a joyful place where people and cats live happily."

1.8m Width Home
866 sq ft

**YUUA Architects
and Associates**

Tokyo, Japan

© Sobajima, Toshihiro

In tall, narrow buildings, the inclusion of natural ventilation minimizes the need for air conditioning, freeing up space while insuring the inhabitant is comfortable.

The correct choice of colors is essential. Warm colors help to provide greater depth, thus alleviating the psychological pressures of compact spaces.

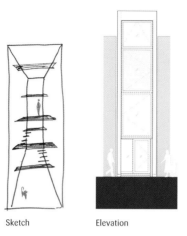

Sketch

Elevation

Section

A. Washroom
B. Bathroom
C. Terrace
D. Loft
E. Living/Dining room/Kitchen
F. Study space
G. Bedroom
H. Entrance
I. Storage

Fist floor plan

Roof plan

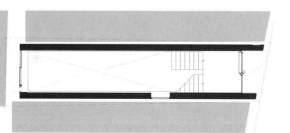

Upper basement floor plan

Third floor plan

Lower basement floor plan

Second floor plan

108

Bathrooms in small houses need to be completely functional, contain all necessary elements, and make the most of the available space.

This project involves the extension and renovation of a 1920s house. Moreover, it represents a victory over housing space limitations.

The extension is a striking shape made of concrete as a continuation of the main house, doubling the height of the space: in the interior, as a double-height room that serves as a rehearsal room for the owners; and in the exterior as a deep parking space. In the main house, a sturdy wooden structure supports two new mezzanines, arising from the demolition of the previous roof and defined by color.

House extension
1,044 sq ft

Benjamin Clarens & Yann Martin/CUT architectures

Chaville, France

© Luc Boegly, David Foessel

109

Combining white or light colors with brighter ones in well-defined areas of a room is another way of increasing the feeling of space.

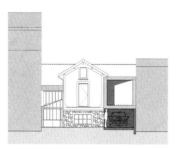

South elevation

North elevation

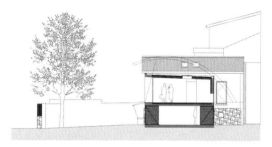

Longitudinal section

Cross section

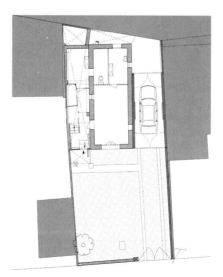

Ground floor plan

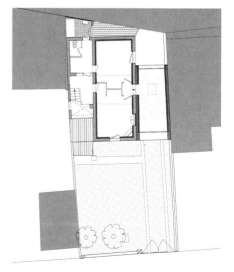

First floor plan

The inner surfaces of the concrete roof, which follows the shape of the southern façade, are coated with a layer of anodized aluminum.

Healdsburg House
912 sq ft

Amy A. Alper, Architect

Healdsburg, California,
United States

© Eric Rorer

In a charming street in Healdsburg, a dilapidated cottage caught the imagination of a couple from Boston.

By reusing the structure and foundations, they managed to create a two-bedroom house. In its new form, the renovated property completely blurs the dividing line between inside and out. It establishes a strong link between open-air and interior spaces, considering both to be as important as each other.

South elevation

East elevation

North elevation

West elevation

Section

110

A small garden or terrace next to the house that acts as an immediate extension of the interior area not only adds extra space, it increases the general feeling of spaciousness.

Existing floor plan

A. Garage
B. Covered
   breezeway
C. Toilet
D. Kitchen
E. Bedroom

F. Driveway
G. Entry
H. Living/Dining
   room
I. Bathroom

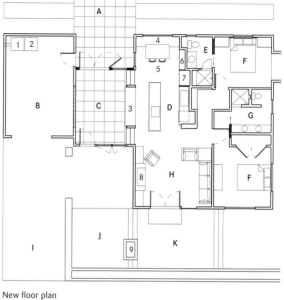

New floor plan

A. Backyard patio
B. Garage
C. Entry/Flex space
D. Kitchen
E. Bathroom
F. Bedroom
G. Master bathroom
H. Living room

I. Driveway
J. Outdoor dining
   room
K. Outdoor living
   room

1. Washer
2. Dryer

3. Bench
4. Banquette
5. Dinette
6. Pantry
7. Fridge
8. Fireplace
9. Fire pit

111

Light furniture with slender legs and panels that are narrow or made of glass makes rooms more airy and help to visually enhance the feeling of space.

112

In continuous spaces, a step
can help to elegantly and
simply differentiate rooms
and their functions, without
wasting any space.

The kitchen design helps the interior to flow smoothly—a simple path circulates from the living room to the kitchen, with the island as a reference.

113

Putting a bench under a large window creates an extra seating area, increases storage space, and establishes a connection between the room and the exterior.

The remodeling of this house pursues a correct reinterpretation of the traditional Singapore "Shophouse."

It is the result of architectural and urban speculation about the different interpretive strategies that, in a modern and meaningful way, can be adopted in a city with a tropical climate. It is an architectural and spatial intervention that affects the style of the building and acknowledges the particular tropical climate and strong historical social significance of these buildings, while at the same time accommodating a modern lifestyle.

Joo Chiat Shophouse
1,823 sq ft

CHANG Architects
Singapore
© Tan Kah Heng

Accommodating the kitchen and a long dining room, the ground floor achieves a connection with the neighborhood and succeeds in retaining one of the most beautiful characteristics of the traditional shophouse.

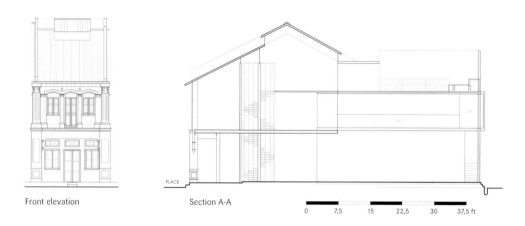

Front elevation

Section A-A

0   7,5   15   22,5   30   37,5 ft

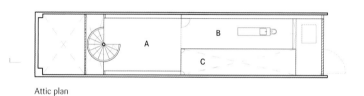

Attic plan

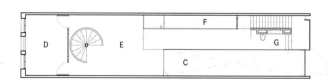

Second floor plan

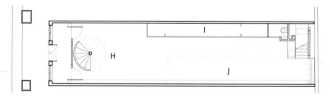

First floor plan

A. Bedroom
B. Outdoor bathroom
C. Courtyard
D. Study
E. Lounge
F. Wardrobes/ Cabinets
G. Bathroom
H. Stairs
I. Kitchen cabinets
J. Courtyard/ Dining room

114

Thanks to their vertical orientation, spiral staircases make the most of the available space, and thanks to their visual strength can also act as a focal point in any environment.

115

In warm climates, an outdoor bathroom gives an extra functionality to an area of the house that otherwise would not exist.

Perched on a slightly sloping corner plot, this house has extensive views of the sky and plenty of natural light all day long.

In residential areas, it is rarely possible to benefit from natural light the whole day, however, this house does not get dark by day, and thanks to the beautifully worked vertical lattice in the ceiling, it also manages to create an additional light reserve that reflects the daily transition of the light and enables the inhabitants to feel the richness and fluidity of the passing of time inside the house.

Koro House
1,155 sq ft

**Katsutoshi Sasaki
+ Associates**

Toyota, Japan

© Katsutoshi Sasaki
+ Associates

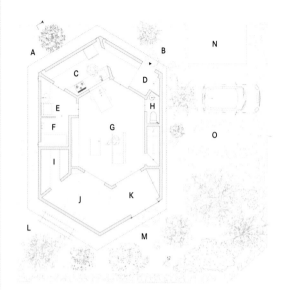

Site plan/First floor

Second floor plan

Loft plan

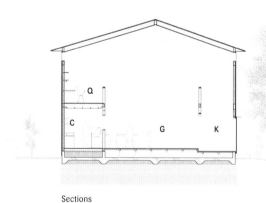

Sections

A. Small private garden	G. Lounge	N. Storage container
B. Approach	H. Toilet	O. Parking
C. Kitchen	I. Walk-in closet	P. Void
D. Entrance	J. Master bedroom	Q. Study space
E. Sanitary	K. Guest room	R. Bedroom
F. Bathroom	L. Laundry garden	S. Loft
	M. Family garden	

116

Straight lines are best in small spaces, as curves create a feeling of heaviness. Straight lines are better at defining spaces, as well as helping to expand and clearly define the internal flow.

The house is perched on the edge of a very steep plot and offers superb views over the city of Nagoya. Its construction was a major challenge given that there was barely enough flat space to park a car, let alone build a house. The design solves this problem by excavating the ground and inserting part of the house into the hillside, with the rest suspended in a stunning cantilever over the slope. The design is completed with the beautiful, original silhouette, shaped like a tent that is about to collapse.

K House
962 sq ft

Akinori Yoshimura, Maki Yoshimura/D.I.G Architects

Nagoya City, Japan

© Maziar Behrooz, Dalto Portella, Francine Fleischer

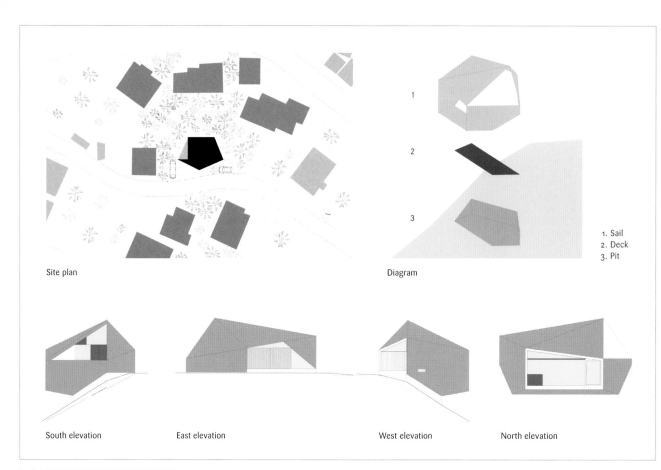

Site plan

Diagram

1. Sail
2. Deck
3. Pit

South elevation

East elevation

West elevation

North elevation

117

Don't put limits on design. This will enable you to create a beautiful and original home, and get the most out of a plot whose orographic conditions or small size is not ideal.

The folded galvanized steel cladding covers both the roof and the walls of the façade, making this tiny home look like a tent from the street.

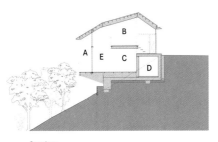

Section

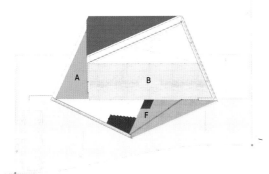

Second floor plan

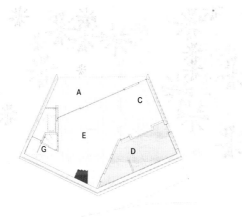

First floor plan

A. Terrace
B. Space 2
C. Kitchen
D. Space 1
E. Living/Dining room
F. Entrance
G. Bathroom

A wooden deck, separated by a large glass wall, extends from the main living-dining space and offers a panoramic view of the city to the front, and of the adjacent fields below.

118

Achieving the right combination of color between different surfaces can enhance the feeling of space. Another option, which not only enhances space but adds beauty and warmth, is to combine wood on the floor with white on the walls and ceilings.

119

In small houses where walls have been removed to increase space, it is important that the bathroom be properly located, as it is generally a room that is highly differentiated from the rest of the space.

This architectural intervention transformed a residential duplex into a single house through the complete reorganization of the interior and the construction of 430 additional square feet on the back.

As a beacon of innovation and dynamism, the extension dominates this typical Montreal street and, in contrast to the main façade, willingly embraces bright colors, angular shapes, and generous glazing. Inside, the wood of the walls and wooden beams is exposed and stands out thanks to the use of a subtle palette in the additional materials.

8th ave
1,630 sq ft

_naturehumaine

Montreal, Quebec, Canada

© Adrien Williams

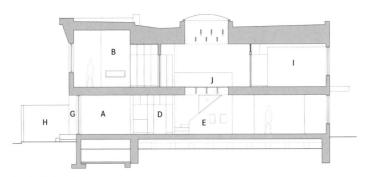

Longitudinal section

Ground floor plan

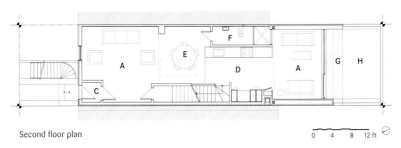

Second floor plan

0   4   8   12 ft

A. Living room   F. Bathroom
B. Master bedroom   G. Patio
C. Vestibule   H. Backyard
D. Kitchen   I. Bedroom
E. Dining room   J. Glass floor

120

The variety of materials, such as glass and lacquer, that is now available for use in the design of kitchen furniture provides plenty of options for finishes that increase the feeling of space.

In a nod to the history of the house, reclaimed wooden slats were used to create a beautiful, warm wooden wall that acts as a backdrop to the stairs, and beams used as a decorative element in the skylight.

121

Transparent glass or plastic floors not only help to differentiate spaces, but they also keep them visually united. For this reason they are an interesting way of increasing the sense of space.

122

A good way of gaining maximum storage space in the bathroom is to use a cabinet with integrated sink. This makes the most of space that otherwise might not be taken into account.

Marlborough House
2,100 sq ft

superkül inc | architect

Toronto, Ontario, Canada

© Tom Arban

With its small rooms, dark finishes, and lack of natural light, the renovation of this early-twentieth-century narrow terraced house focused on creating a cleaner and lighter space through the elaborate balancing of cost, aesthetics, and sustainability.

In an increasingly urbanized population, this project reinterprets the traditional house, accommodating in a more fluid way family dynamics and work patterns. The result is a fine example of a strategic approach to urban regeneration.

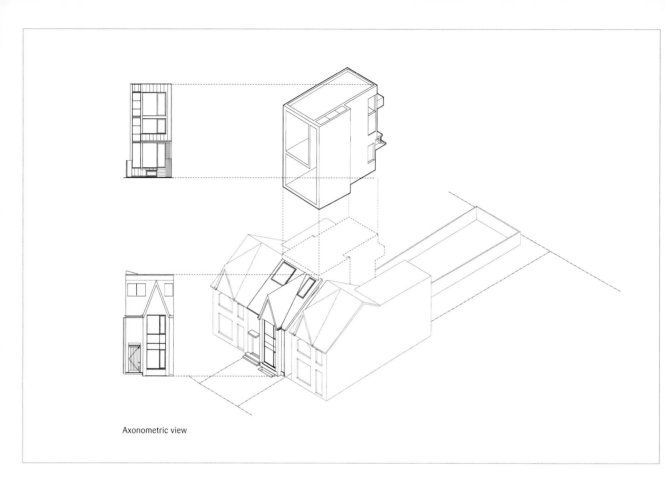

Axonometric view

123

In very narrow houses, organizing activities in parallel spaces, from the communal areas to the private zones, is a good way of distributing the rooms.

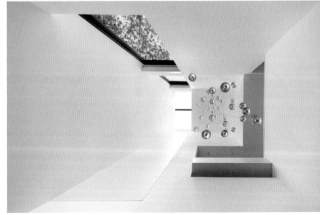

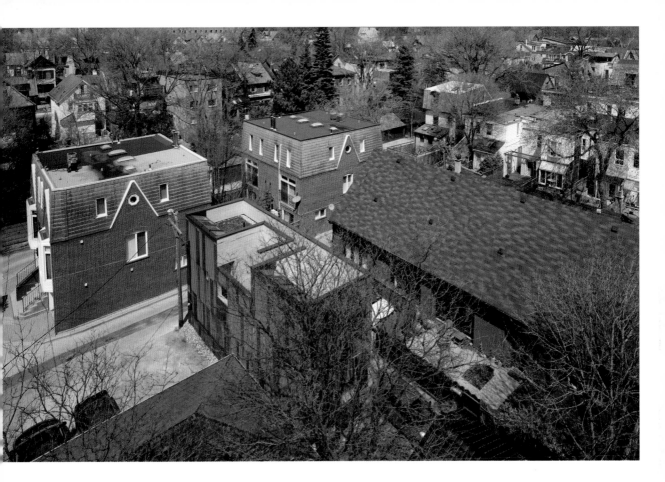

Superkül transformed this old warehouse into a family home right in the heart of Toronto. This project addresses questions such as sustainability and urban regeneration, the density of the city's narrow streets, and the limited living space, all with a limited budget and resources.

The resulting reconstruction provides the building with all the comforts you need in a home—outdoor space, natural light, and a well-designed living area—while retaining much of the existing industrial character on the outside.

40R Laneway House
850 sq ft

superkül inc | architect

Toronto, Ontario, Canada

© Tom Arban

The steel casing of the original building
was catalogued, removed, restored, and
reinstalled as its main skin.

124

When there is a shortage of windows, try to draw attention to the highest part of the house, from which significant amounts of natural light can be obtained, and sufficient ventilation achieved.

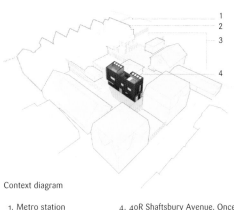

Context diagram

1. Metro station
2. Single family residential
3. 1880–1982: Industrial use zone/1992–: Residential conversion
4. 40R Shaftsbury Avenue. Once a smithy, later a horse shed, hotel storage, a taxi depot and an artist studio, today this laneway house stands as a private residence and a model for sustainable urban living

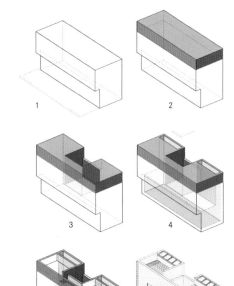

1. Existing building mass. Ceiling heights—8' + 6', building 17' cantilever added circa 1950
2. Vertical expansion. By-laws restrict horizontal expansion; bldg. height response, raise to 23'
3. Second floor contract. Courtyard added to bring light and air into second floor
4. Light shafts. Vertical light shafts, 23', bring light to first floor
5. Rooftop terrain. Right-of-way restricts development of landscape terrace and planting added to rooftop
6. Cladding. Refurbished cladding systems mimic original industrial skins – wood + metal

Axonometric diagrams

■ Horizontal expansion
■ Courtyard
Light shaft
Green roof

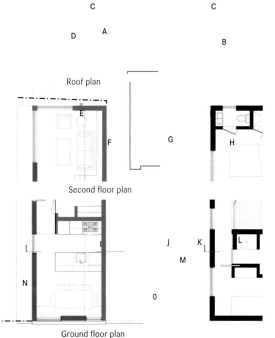

Roof plan

Second floor plan

Ground floor plan

East-west section

A. Terrace
B. Green roof
C. Skylight vents
D. Planter
E. Light shaft
F. Principal bedroom
G. Elevated courtyard
H. Bedroom
I. Living room
J. Mechanical room
K. Kitchen
L. Dining room
M. Hallway
N. Neighbouring garage
O. Right-of-way

125

Besides being a suitable solution for use in densely populated urban areas, tiny houses can also be used to transform old industrial areas into residential zones.

Anywhere
Modular/Prefabricated

Blob vB3
215 sq ft

dmvA

Anywhere

© Frederik Vercruysse

This project originated as a house extension that, due to legal regulations, was eventually transformed into an original mobile home. Despite its striking silhouette, this "space-egg" has everything that its inhabitants could need: bathroom, kitchen, lighting, a bed, and shelves on which to store their belongings. Furthermore, as if its residential credentials were not enough, it can also be used as an office, guesthouse, reception, garden shed, or for any other imaginable function. It has completely evolved from its original idea.

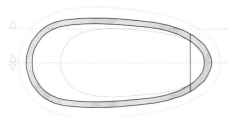

Floor plan

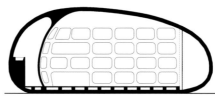

Central vertical section 1

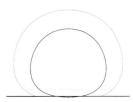

Front outline

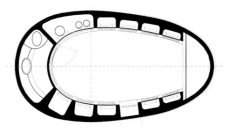

Horizontal section at height 120

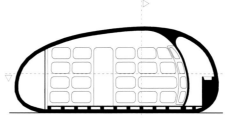

Central vertical section 2

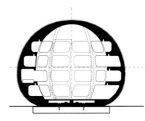

Cross section

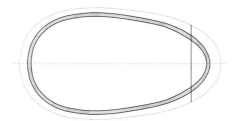

Horizontal section at height 170

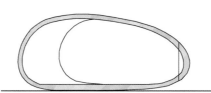

Vertical section at height 75

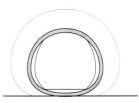

Cross section at nose

126

A space more or less the size of a large caravan is ideal for small mobile homes. At this size, the house can be adapted to any location.

127

Open shelving, set into nooks
and crannies and occupying
most of the wall space, can
provide huge storage space
in tiny homes.

128

Using a pivoting door is a very interesting option in small houses: it saves space, provides dual access to the area beyond, and is undeniably beautiful.

In 2012, Kris and Griet bought, for just 15 euros, a construction trailer that was being disposed of by the local town hall. Their idea was to use it as a place in which they and their two children could relax, play, and study. Two years later, with the help of architect Karel, the project came to fruition.

Once the old fittings had been removed and replaced, the trailer was transformed into a tiny home that was almost unrecognizable from the original and that, thanks to its versatile design, is able to fulfill its owners' original wishes.

Werfkeet
86 sq ft

Karel Verstraeten

Vlimmeren, Belgium

© FELT

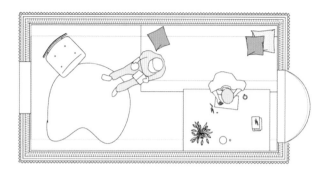

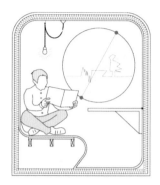

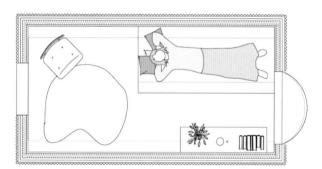

Drawings

129

Spatial versatility—the possibility of having different options for the location of interior elements—is essential in order not to affect the dynamics of the inhabitants.

The large circular opening in the wall-mounted skylight is the main source of natural light, and provides sweeping views of the surrounding terrain.

Interior diagrams

This prototype is a transportable modular housing project, which can be fully produced in the city in just six weeks and moved to wherever you wish to install it.

From beginning to end, this project is enormously versatile. Even online, the client can configure their own home based on different module options, using a system that connects the modules and requires no further instructions if they wish to add more spaces now or in the future.

Remote House
861 sq ft

Felipe Assadi
Pichicuy, Chile
© Fernando Alda

130

Integrating your appliances into the kitchen furniture is essential for maximizing space. Furthermore, it also creates a sense of order and organization, which is essential in a working area such as the kitchen.

131

Despite their space limitations, modular homes usually offer other advantages. They are quick to construct, easy to transport, and can be installed almost anywhere.

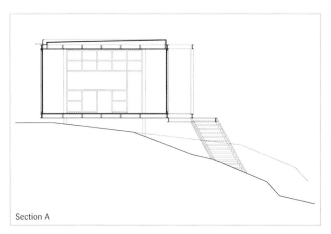

Section A

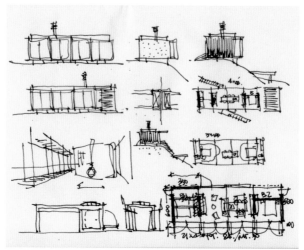

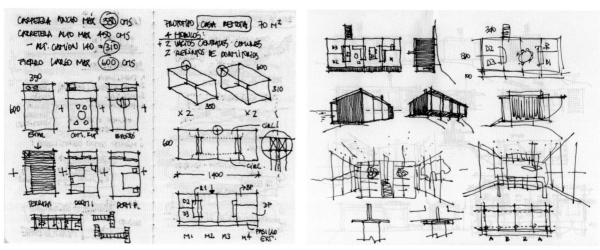

Sketches

The frame of the house is made of iron. Pinewood is used to clad the outside and the walls, floor, and ceiling of the interior.

Rock Reach Dos
1,500 sp ft

02 Architecture

Yucca Valley, California,
United States

© NuVue Interactive

Situated in a remote, hard-to-access area of great natural
beauty, this prefabricated steel home is a modest residence
that has very low environmental impact and requires very little
maintenance.

Thanks to the speed and efficiency of the prefabrication
process, the house was built in just eight weeks and
created very little waste, as the construction materials and
prefabricated elements were transported ready to be installed
in their chosen plot.

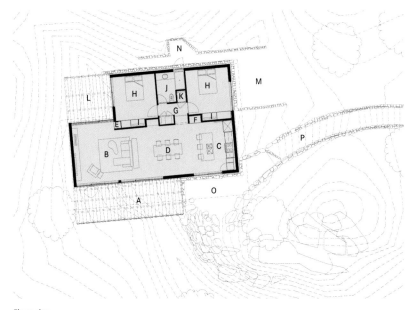

Floor plan

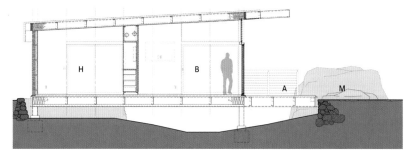

Section

A. Balcony
B. Living room
C. Kitchen
D. Dining room
E. Audiovisual
F. Pantry
G. Vestibule
H. Bedroom
I. Closet
J. Bathroom
K. Laundry
L. Deck
M. Patio
N. Outdoor shower
O. Entry patio
P. Foot path

The house is suspended over the
ground on cold-formed, light-gauge
steel columns and beams. The cladding
consists of a grid of prefabricated panels
and standard construction elements.

132

The latest construction techniques and materials, previously used only in the building of traditional houses, are now frequently used in the construction of modular homes.

133

In the bathroom, the most efficient and space-saving solution is to use spotlights embedded in the ceiling, combined with one or more lights in the mirror.

L-shaped MIMA
388 sq ft per module

Mário Rebelo de Sousa

Brejos da Carregueira, Portugal

© José Campos

This house is a sharp white shape which, even amid the beautiful landscapes of the Alentejo, stands out for its originality and elegance.

This summer home is just one example of the multiple configuration schemes that can be developed from a single common base. MIMA basic units of 388 square feet are used to develop a prefabricated construction system that allows one to quickly design and produce houses that are completely customizable in their size, spatial organization, and materials, based on a common 5x5 feet structure.

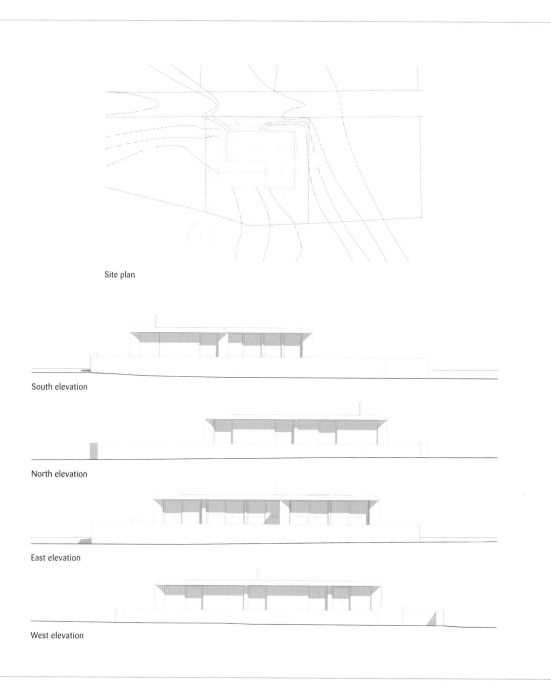

Site plan

South elevation

North elevation

East elevation

West elevation

134

In addition to offering all the advantages of a traditional house, a prefabricated home can be assembled in as little as sixty days.

135

The use of clean, straight lines, light colors, and materials such as wood, plaster, and white tiles in minimalist interiors creates soft and harmonious spaces that are pleasant to live in.

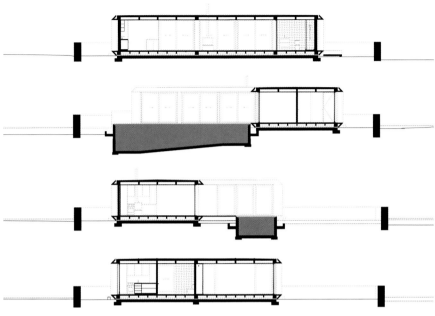

Sections

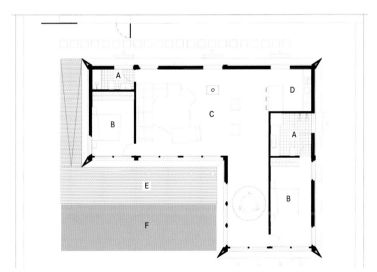

Floor plan

A. Bathroom
B. Bedroom
C. Living room
D. Kitchen
E. Deck
F. Pool

Shelter
592 sq ft

Vipp

Anywhere

© Vipp

This natural plug-and-play haven provides an escape from urban chaos. It is a prefabricated object, designed to the very last detail so that the only thing the client needs to do is decide where to put it.

It starts with the basics, a return to nature in a dense and compact space. The landscape is framed on purpose to make it a dominant element of the interior, where dark tones prevail to keep the focus on nature. The immensity of nature fits inside, and is omnipresent for its inhabitant.

136

When spaces are not just small but are also narrow, large windows not only increase the feeling of space, but also make the house feel permeable, forcefully bringing the outside in.

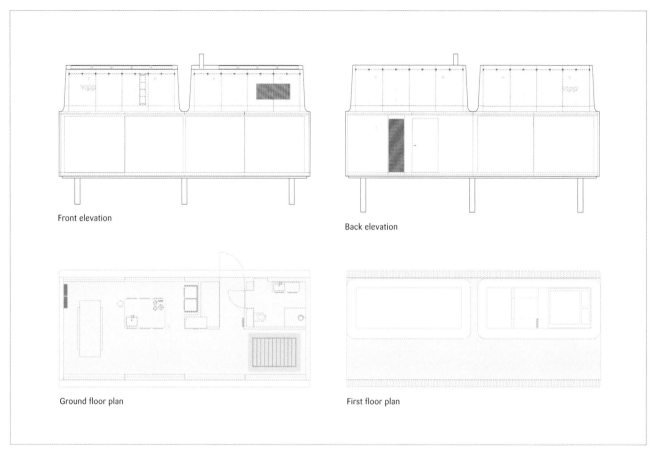

Front elevation

Back elevation

Ground floor plan

First floor plan

The two-story structure is supported
by a simple steel frame, with only the
bathroom and bunk bed isolated from
the main space.

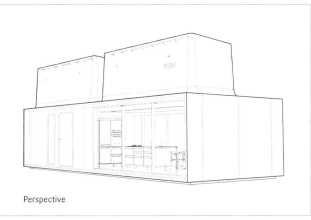

Perspective

The chalet is fully equipped with Vipp products—everything from lighting to bed linen, from the bed to the brush in the bathroom and from the shelves to the soap dispenser.

137

A large bed that takes up
the whole of the bedroom
space is not only comfortable
but also enhances the visual
feeling of space.

Carbon Positive House
570 sq ft

Bill McCorkell

Melbourne, Victoria, Australia

© Tom Ross

With this project, Archiblox has succeeded in developing the world's first carbon-positive house. By uniting sensitive design and new technologies, this house allows the owner to rid himself of the shackles of modern life and benefit from the fact that it generates more energy than it consumes.

The house aims to make a significant contribution to society by addressing environmental problems such as the increased levels of carbon emissions and the high levels of energy consumed in standard-built housing.

This house was designed to be inserted into the ground at the rear, providing greater insulation and regulation of the interior temperature.

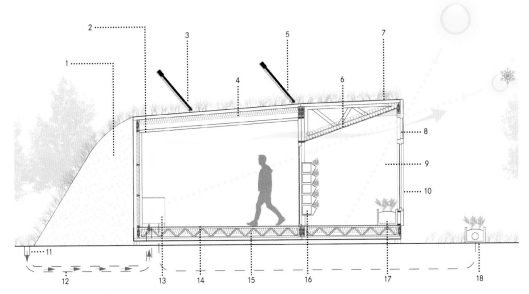

Diagram of eco-sustainable solutions

1. Earth berm wall
2. FSC, Australian-grown EO hoop pine ply internal wall & ceiling lining
3. Solar-evacuated tube hot water system
4. R6 Earthwool insulated batts
5. 5 kW solar PV power system with energy monitoring
6. R6 Earthwool insulated batts
7. Green roof

8. Operable highlight windows for natural convection & circulation
9. UBIQ panel for wall & ceiling lining green house
10. FSC double-glazed timber windows & doors. R2 Earthwool insulation batts
11. Fridge/Freezer ventilation
12. Cool tubes for summer cooling
13. Carbon-neutral internal kitching joinery

14. 16mm UBIQ panel flooring
15. R6 Earthwool insulated batts
16. Green wall plant, herb, & mass wall
17. Modular wicker planter boxes for mass & food production
18. External planter bed to take gray water waste & filter for toilet flushing

138

Sustainable strategies, such as cross-ventilation, solar energy, or green roofs, among others, are perfectly applicable to small-size projects.

Open, fresh, and light-filled spaces are a good example of the best and most innovative contemporary prefabricated house designs.

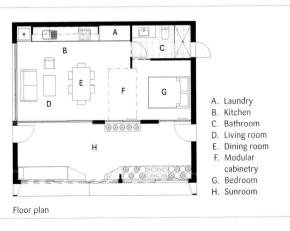

Floor plan

A. Laundry
B. Kitchen
C. Bathroom
D. Living room
E. Dining room
F. Modular cabinetry
G. Bedroom
H. Sunroom

139

The planters installed in the wall of the sunroom create a small garden in which residents can grow herbs and vegetables.

140

If carpentry is used intelligently and the total height of the space is utilized, the house's spatial functionality will never be compromised.

Using an efficient building system and a simplified palette of finishes, the goal of building a house in limited time and with a small budget was realized.

The property combines distinct three-dimensional modules, which in turn are made from panels for floor, walls, and ceilings. Furthermore, the modules are designed in two different widths and heights that combine to create the different areas of the house, each with its own specific function.

House SIP m3
1,668 sq ft

Hsu-Rudolphy Arquitectos

Colina, Chile

© Aryeh Kornfeld,
Skyfilms Chile

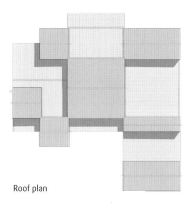

Roof plan

Medium height floor plan

Floor plan

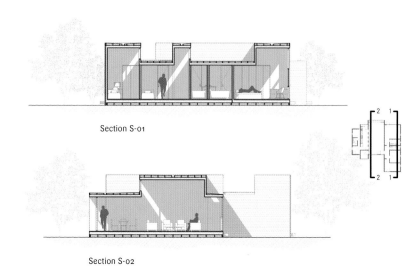

Section S-01

Section S-02

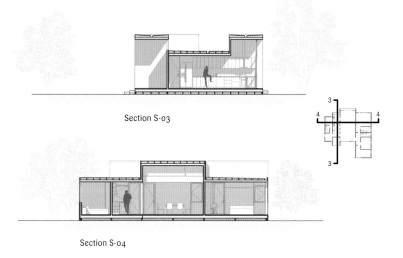

Section S-03

Section S-04

The project is divided into four parallel shapes composed of a collection of modules. The thin modules house the service areas while the wider ones accommodate the communal spaces and bedrooms.

141

Tall houses provide greater interior space without necessarily needing to increase the surface area. Thinking in terms of cubic yards as opposed to square yards is another way of considering the space.

142

Extra storage capacity can be gained by installing kitchen units at two different heights. Opting for a prevalence of straight lines can also create a greater feeling of spaciousness.

Inspired by nature, influenced by modernism, and designed according to the simplicity of a construction game for children, the design is a compact yet extremely comfortable modular living space that is suitable for a wide variety of applications.

The central concept is a collection of standard components that can be connected together to form living modules (cells), which in turn can be connected to other modules to form a group of living modules (a beehive). The result is a simple but modern structure that is affordable, sustainable, flexible, and easy to build.

HIVEHAUS®
100 sq ft per module

Barry Jackson

Anywhere

© Hivehaus

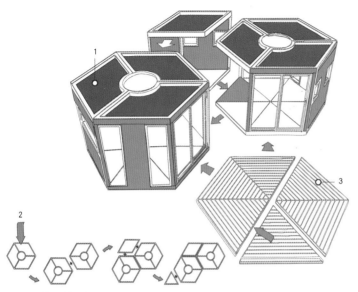

1

2

3

Diagram of modular design

1. Modular: Identically proportioned hexagonal modules can be joined together at any time by any or all of their six sides to create a cluster of connected modules or "Hive"

2. Expandable: Hexagonal modules can be broken down into smaller diamond and triangular modules and combinations of these three simple shapes can provide endless design configurations

3. Decking: Hexagonal decks of the same proportions can be connected via any side to allow external expansion of the "Hive"

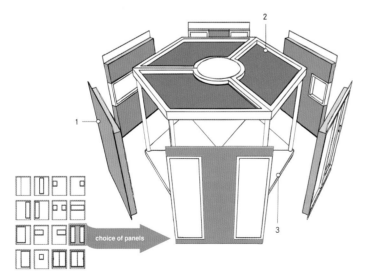

1

2

3

choice of panels

Diagram of modular flexibility

1. Walls/Windows: Choose from a standard selection of interchangeable wall and window panels to create your own individual HIVEHAUS® design

2. Roof: Each roof is constructed from three identical molded GRP sections on top of a structural timber frame

3. Floor: Interconnecting equilateral triangular floor sections tessellate to provide highly flexible design possibilities

The careful sizing of each of the cells that make up this house enables each one to accommodate a full room, be it kitchen, bathroom, or bedroom.

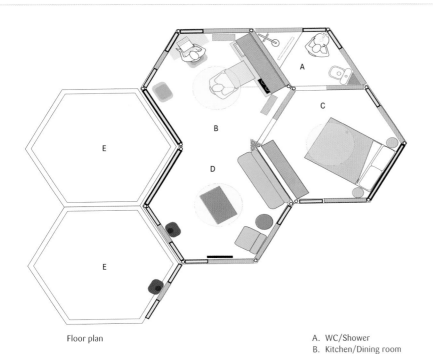

Floor plan

A. WC/Shower
B. Kitchen/Dining room
C. Bedroom
D. Lounge
E. Decking

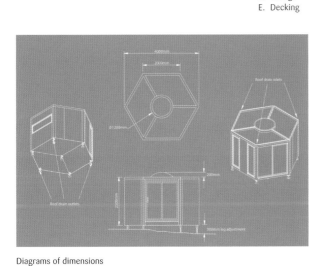

Diagrams of dimensions

143

A wireless LED lighting system is suitable for use in modular homes. It dispenses with cables, and the switches can be located according to the final distribution of the modules.

144

In modular homes composed of several units, each unit takes on a specific use that is differentiated from the others: office, kitchen, bedroom, bathroom, and so on.

Marfa Weehouse
585 sq ft

Alchemy

Marfa, Texas, United States

© Scott Ervin

The client wanted a house of modest size, which would sit lightly on a remote plot, twenty minutes from the small artist colony of Marfa, Texas.

The prefabricated home comprises a total of three modules; however, the interior and exterior of the first module to be installed are completely finished and there is even an outdoor shed. Alchemy has created a new ideal of luxury based on size, a way of leveraging the uniqueness of the site through the multiple use of space and a simplicity and elegance in its detail.

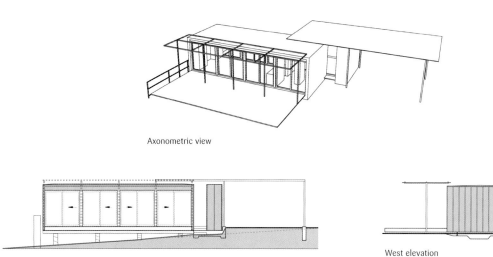

Axonometric view

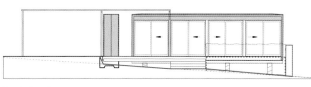

South elevation

West elevation

North elevation

West elevation

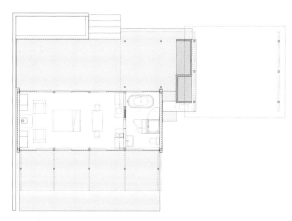

Floor plan

Large terraces encourage outdoor living; the windows provide natural cross-ventilation while large awnings block the intense sun of southwestern Texas.

145

A fireplace in a small house can generate enough heat to warm the entire space, even though other complementary forms of heating may be installed.

146

Appliances that are in the
same material or color as the
rest of the kitchen cabinets
bring a sense of continuity
to the furniture, and thus a
greater sense of space.

Rock Reach
1,000 sq ft

02 Architecture

Yucca Valley, California,
United States

© NuVue Interactive

This house is the result of a collaboration between 02
Architecture and the prefabricated home developer Blue Sky
Homes, and was inspired by Le Corbusier's DOM-INO house.
It contains a pure structure of columns and levels, making
it highly adaptable as the walls are not load bearing and the
openings can be located freely within the structure to meet the
varying requirements of the site.

As a model for a future line of prefabricated houses, it is fully
sustainable and can be completely dismantled and relocated
wherever desired.

147

Although they tend to be small, the inherent nature of prefabricated houses promotes sustainability, as they use little energy and minimize waste.

148

Technology can be a great ally in small spaces. Modern consumer electronics such as flat-screen TVs, which are now so common, can help to save space.

149

In tiny houses that have done away with interior walls in order to maximize space, good furniture distribution is essential for defining the different areas and the functions that they are used for.

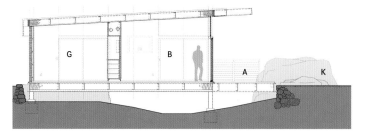

Section

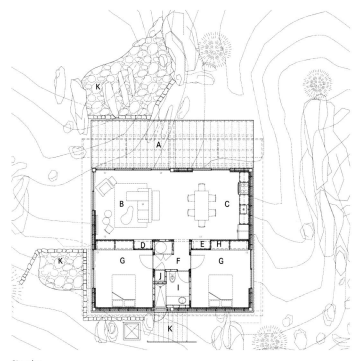

Site plan

A. Balcony
B. Living room
C. Kitchen
D. Audiovisual
E. Pantry
F. Vestibule
G. Bedroom
H. Closet
I. Bathroom
J. Laundry
K. Patio

This house is the result of collaboration between furniture designers and architects, a meeting point in which to experiment with ideas that are on the cusp of architecture and industrial design, where low-impact materials are combined, using 3D printing techniques for the prefabrication of structures to ensure higher quality and better economy in the use of materials.

The result is a multipurpose house that responds both to growing families and to their recreational requirements through three functional modes: open, play, and sleep.

Bigwin Island Bunkie
300 sq ft

BLDG Workshop Inc. + 608 Design = The Bunkie Co.

Toronto, Ontario, Canada

© The Bunkie Co.

This project is a collaboration between
furniture manufacturers Evan Bare of
608 Design and Jim Moore, together
with Jorge Torres and Nathan Buhler
of BLDG Workshop.

150

Using the same finish
throughout the interior,
such as the use of paint of the
same color or type, eliminates
contrast, thus enhancing the
feeling of space.

DIRECTORY

Alchemy
Saint Paul, Minnesota, United States
www.weehouse.com

Amy A. Alper, Architect
Sonoma, California, United States
www.alperarchitect.com

Andrew Maynard Architects
Melbourne, Victoria, Australia
www.maynardarchitects.com

Anonymous Architects
Los Angeles, California, United States
www.anonymousarchitects.com

Bill McCorkell/Archiblox
Burnley, Victoria, Australia
www.archiblox.com.au

Gabriela Kapralova/ASGK Design
Prague, Czech Republic
www.asgk.cz

Bates Masi + Architects
Sag Harbor, New York, United States
www.batesmasi.com

benn + penna architecture
Pyrmont, New South Wales, Australia
www.bennandpenna.com

BLDG Workshop
Toronto, Ontario, Canada
www.bldgworkshop.ca

Bloem en Lemstra Architecten
Amsterdam, the Netherlands
www.bnla.nl

Castanes Architects
Seattle, Washington, United States
www.castanes.com

Castroferro Arquitectos
Vigo, Spain
www.castroferro.com

CHANG Architects
Singapore, Singapore
www.changarch.com

CUT architectures
Paris, France
www.cut-architectures.com

D.I.G Architects
Nagoya, Japan
www.dig-arch.com

dmvA
Mechelen, Belgium
www.dmva-architecten.be

Pablo Serrano Elorduy/dom arquitectura
Barcelona, Spain
www.dom-arquitectura.com

FAM Architekti
Prague, Czech Republic
www.famarchitekti.cz

Felipe Assadi Arquitectos
Santiago de Chile, Chile
www.felipeassadi.com

**Karel Verstraeten/
FELT architecture & design**
Ghent, Belgium
www.felt.works

Fujiwaramuro Architects
Osaka, Japan
www.aplan.jp

Hiroyuki Shinozaki Architects
Tokyo, Japan
www.shnzk.com

Barry Jackson/HIVEHAUS®
Wigan, United Kingdom
www.hivehaus.co.uk

Horibe Associates architect's office
Osaka, Japan
www.horibeassociates.com

Hsu-Rudolphy Arquitectos
Santiago de Chile, Chile
www.gabrielrudolphy.cl

Jacobs Chang Architecture
New York, New York, United States
www.jacobschang.com

Jarmund/Vigsnæs AS Arkitekter MNAL
Oslo, Norway
www.jva.no

Jeffery S. Poss, Architect
Champaign, Illinois, United States
www.jefferyspossarchitect.net

Johnsen Schmaling Architects
Milwaukee, Wisconsin, United States
www.johnsenschmaling.com

Katsutoshi Sasaki + Associates
Toyota, Japan
www.sasaki-as.com

LASC studio
Copenhagen, Denmark
www.lascstudio.com

Lode Architecture
Paris, France
www.lode-architecture.com

mA-style architects
Shizuoka, Japan
www.ma-style.jp

Marte.Marte.Architekten
Weiler, Austria
www.marte-marte.com

Mason & Wales Architects
Dunedin, Otago, New Zealand
www.masonandwales.com

Mário Rebelo de Sousa/MIMA Lab
Viana do Castelo, Portugal
www.mimahousing.com

Modostudio
Roma, Italy
www.modostudio.eu

**Jorge Palomo Carmona/
Modulo 12 Arquitectos**
Madrid, Vigo, Gijón; Spain
www.modulo12.org

Mork Ulnes Architects
San Francisco, California, United States
www.morkulnes.com

Nan Arquitectos
Pontevedra, Spain
www.nanarquitectos.com

_naturehumaine
Montreal, Quebec, Canada
www.naturehumaine.com

02 Architecture
Palm Springs, California, United States
www.o2arch.com

Olson Kundig Architects
Seattle, Washington, United States
www.olsonkundig.com

Panorama
Santiago de Chile, Chile
www.panoramaarquitectos.com

Philip Stejskal Architecture
Perth, Western Australia, Australia
www.architectureps.com

Raum
Nantes, France
www.raum.fr

rzlbd
Toronto, Ontario, Canada
www.rzlbd.com

Satish Jassal Architects
London, United Kingdom
www.satishjassal.co.uk

Scott & Scott Architects
Vancouver, British Columbia, Canada
www.scottandscott.ca

SoHo Architektur
Memmingen, Germany
www.soho-architektur.de

Studio Zero85
Montesilvano, Italy
www.studiozero85.com

superkül inc | architect
Toronto, Ontario, Canada
www.superkul.ca

Turnbull Griffin Haesloop
San Francisco, California, United States
www.tgharchitects.com

UNarquitectura
Santiago de Chile, Chile
www.unarquitectura.cl

Vipp
Copenhaguen, Denmark
www.vipp.com

WMR Arquitectos
Santiago de Chile, Chile
www.wmrarq.cl

Yasutaka Yoshimura Architects
Tokyo, Japan
www.ysmr.com

Yoshihiro Yamamoto | YYAA
Osaka, Japan
www.yyaa.jp

YUUA Architects & Associates
Tokyo, Japan
www.yuua.jp

Yuusuke Karasawa Architects
Tokyo, Japan
www.yuusukekarasawa.com